Becoming By Being

BY

DEDE WELDON CASAD, Ph.D

DISCOVERING LIFE'S POTENTIALS TODAY
(Revised Edition)

Table Of Contents

To all becomers...
Some of whom I know and are a part of this book
and some who have added to the fun of my own ongoing "becoming."

ACKNOWLEDGEMENT

Becoming by Being is a book about many people, and in a very real sense they each have been a part of its formation.

There are dear and close friends, who contributed in reading, thinking, and consulting with me through the years of its development. Then there is the 'pilot group,' friends who took the time to participate in weekly meetings over two months to work through the process of validating the idea into a logical program. My thanks to them recurs every time becoming and being occupies my mind.

Then lastly, to my husband and family who lived with me and witnessed for themselves the silent process of one at work with an idea. They all deserve and indeed have my greatest appreciation and love. The measure of patience that I have managed as I have practiced what I have preached in Becoming by Being, I trust served us all well.

INTRODUCTION

*B*ecoming by Being came out in the early 80s, so in editing and revising it I realized much of what was written then is still a clear and relevant message for people today. We still need to understand ourselves and evaluate our motives. And most of all we still need to be fulfilled. No fancy electronic devise can help us in this regard. They can make our activities easier, but they cannot reach into our inner most beings and decide for us. We are still left to our own devises when it comes to learning what it is that makes us who we are, and what we must do to reach our true potential.

The premise of Becoming by Being is simple. It is the art of being today what you wish to become tomorrow. The idea is not new. It is basic learning, but the idea of becoming by being, as a method of achieving the ultimate self, came to me years ago…and this is the story.

It began when I had a visit from an idea. I thought it would pass as many ideas do and I could forget it easily. The idea, nevertheless, lodged. Before I knew it this persistent thought of being a co-creator of my future began to grow and develop and grip my mind. With it I realized I didn't have to accept the fact that natural circumstances would govern my years ahead; I could help design my future and become what I wanted to become by being it right now. To my surprise this idea took charge and soon became powerful enough to direct my life.

When this thought came, I was in the midst of the empty-nest crisis. At the time, it was the "in" thing to have a crisis of a personal nature: an identity crisis, a marital crisis or a job crisis. On Wednesday mornings, car pools headed for the psychiatrist's office: town hall meetings were repeatedly scheduled and the family health clinics were blooming. The ink from each new book on creative problem solving hardly dried before the book was seized by the hungry do-it-yourself public.

My empty-nest crisis came at the same time the Women's Lib movement began changing women's names and I realized, since they were rearranging my name, I might as well take a look at my identity.

By name, serial number or finger prints I knew I had an identity. I grew up with the word. My generation originated the Driver's License, the Social Security Card and the Zip Code. Yet, Erik Erickson says, "Identity is a term alternately circumscribing something so large and seemingly self-evident that to demand a definition would almost seem petty." Yet demand it, I did.

When addressing a seminar in Florida several years ago the late Bishop Fulton Sheen asked a startling question. "Why is it that people, after twenty or thirty years, wonder who they are? How did we ever get into this problem of identity anyway?" He suggests that it arises when we have no limits and no boundaries, and he illustrated his theory by pointing to the State of Florida. "How do we know, for example, the identity of the State of Florida?" he asked. "By its boundaries. How do we know the identity of a basketball court or a football field? By their boundaries." He concluded that "as soon as we lose our boundaries and limits we have a problem with identity."

My own boundaries and limits were measured by my understanding of my own being. For forty years I busied myself in being but my being-ness hinged on what others wanted and needed me to be. It was a pattern predesigned and precut by a larger family called society. No wife, mother, social involver or church worker fit the prototype of society's expectations more than I. I measured up. Those first years I scored as a passable be-er and today I'm passably proud of my being. No apologies and few regrets. Yet today I find myself slipping out of my boundaries, questioning the world out there—that world of so-called potential, fulfillment and wholeness. I want to know, for myself, what these words mean and if these qualities hold within them a new identity for me--for all of us—an identity we can have some say-so about. This calls for value clarification, and some simple homework with the dictionary.

"Potential," says Herbert Otto, "is that within you called the undiscovered self." He suggests that there are hidden or dormant capacities, abilities, talents and resources that all persons possess but haven't gotten around to developing. When I looked the word up in the dictionary, I found potential to mean "that which is possible as opposed to the actual—yet capable of being and becoming.

It was being what and becoming what, using what capabilities, what hidden abilities, what dormant talents and resources that lodged like a log jam in my head.

From that muddle, the idea of becoming by being began to break loose. I thought of it, at first, in simple terms—as the art of becoming by the act of being, then as a way of changing my future. It pressed persistently for my attention and finally my total commitment, not only in an intellectual way, but lived out in daily affairs. The idea soon became the beginning of a venture as surprising and as encompassing as the discovery of a new world.

I became interesting in becoming, not as a dreamer, fantasizing about being a "somebody." I already was a somebody with full credentials regarding body, mind and spirit. Nor was I interested in becoming a famous personage with my name as familiar as our morning cereal. These were not for me.

I was interested rather, in exploring what I had been led to believe was my unique potential. The potential that precedes wholeness. I was convinced there was more to me and I wanted to get at it while I had the time, the good health and the desire to complete the task. I didn't want to die before I discovered, for myself, all that was bottled up in my special and peculiar formula.

I was interested in how others like me, my associates at the office, my neighbors, my parents before me and my three children after me, might stretch out to the ultimate of their intended being. If the aim of life is to be fully born, as Erich Fromm suggests and our basic duty to be alive is the same as the duty to become oneself, I realized I had work to do. One doesn't reenter the womb, as Nicodemus learned, rather one relies on a thorough re-evaluation of the birth process in the light of this new knowledge. Then one concludes that every day is a new beginning, every experience a new chapter, and that a birth explanation is more a process of becoming than a one time event.

So the becoming I seek is the becoming that is to be achieved in being all that I am intended to be. And the method I have begun to follow is the only method I know: to learn by doing and to become by being.

Doggedly, this idea stayed with me, hosting every move and monitoring every thought and before long I ceased treating it as a visitor and began to welcome it as a companion. I toyed with it, played with it and used all manner of means to develop and perfect it. I was it carrier and it, in turn, carried me into exciting daily interplays of growing. It stretched me, it refined me and brought me a deeper understanding of myself and the operational world around me.

Today, I marvel at what one idea can do to change a person's life—holding it captive, as this idea did me, until it uses the person to its own end; suggesting, prodding, goading, almost to the degree of forcing its way with one. A good idea is not to be denied, I learned, especially if its time has come and its victim vulnerable.

"I should not talk so much about myself if there were anybody else whom I knew as well," confessed Thoreau. This book is freckled with the pronoun I and I would be given to telling the story in another way if I knew how. As it is, I am guardian and trustee of an idea until I bring you in on it. The over used "I" then is employed not in the sense of "do as I do" —but rather, as the starting runner in a relay race.

Learning, the process of becoming by being, I hope to hand you the stick as I come around and then cheer you on, as you discover further possibilities of becoming in your own life. Believe me, it's no spectator sport; however, if you, like the young man commenting on a college course, "it'll be a snap, that is—unless I get interested," find the concept captivating, you may, as I am doing, make of it an intellectual hobby. For myself, I now consider becoming by being an intellectual hobby of self-actualization. Understanding that a hobby is an activity or interest pursued for pleasure and relaxation and not a main occupation, I can honestly say that now my only hobby is me.

I may be the first person in captivity to publicly admit that startling confession, but I feel, unless a person is six feet under standard, he above all others, is fascinated by his own thoughts and mystified by his inconsistent behavior.

The interest in ourselves is so fundamental it is foursquare, yet we try to make others believe, by our false faces and clumsy facades; that our interest in ourselves is of little concern. Modesty forbid! Under the guise of wanting to know more about ourselves, we storm the bookstores, and snatch up every leaflet and pamphlet that might shed light on our confusing natures. We rush to enroll in courses which deal with "Coping with Stress," "Biofeedback Training," "Getting It All Together: Mind, Body and Spirit." We take up new and bizarre methods of self-improvement and we flip through magazines taking tests on "Is Our Marriage Successful?" or "Can My Personality Be Improved?"

And why not? Each life is a novel, a story, unique and untold, grist for the pen. You and I are the stuff of which history is made and from whom great works of literature emerge. What goes on in the mind is such a mystery that we gladly place ourselves on the firing line and allow all manner of attacks to fill us with holes, hoping we can learn about ourselves from the bleeding.

That makes my hobby your hobby. You are interested in me for what you can learn about yourself and I am interested in you for what I can learn about myself.

Naturally!

We are all compost piles, a motley mixture of organic, pedantic, erratic, fanatic and ecstatic energies. We show kindness to a neighbor one minute and scream at the kids the next; to one person we may appear aloof, to another show the finest expression of warmth and consideration. In some situations we act stable, mature and use good judgment. In others, we falter and stammer to overcome fears and frustrations. On occasion we are self-confident, self-possessed and comfortably secure; on others, we crawl back into our hell-holes of anxiety, insecurity and ulcer ridden complexities. On our better days we are happy, buoyant, creative and can cope. On other days we are slow, critical and verging on tears.

If this is the stuff of Being, then Being has some exciting implications. If this is the stuff of which Becoming is made, then it is even more enticing. From these rag bags of unrefined qualities comes the need for unity, consistency and wholeness. We can't sew new patches on old wine skins any longer.

As a hobby of any other kind, the process would be the same. I don't work with wood, but they tell me that master craftsmen take the raw material, cut and saw, hammer and nail, stick and glue, and paint and polish until the work of art is perfected. The pleasure they receive is not only the result of their work, though that is what the public views as beautiful and lasting, the pleasure is in the process—the development of the art itself, working through the various stages toward completion. I feel it can be this way with each of us. When one takes himself, not seriously, but studiously, one takes the raw, unmolded material and puts it through the developmental process of becoming.

So my hobby is not unique, nor do I think it narcissistic. I think it is universal. We are all alike, we say, and human nature never changes. Maybe not. But human beings can. This is why I became a deliberate becomer..

ONE STEP AT A TIME

"It isn't enough to take steps which may some day lead to a goal; each step must be itself a goal," says Goethe. Those who seek instant conversion or urgent transformation in their personal lives may quickly put this book aside and go back to the stacks. This book is not a quick-fix for change. One will not find in it means and methods of radical surgery, tearing the self from the body in order to clean it out or clean it up or make it new again.

It is neither a motor overhaul nor a deep pile vacuum designed to do the job in a day's time. It is a book of ordinary becomers— those who cast the long look before their lives and seek, with some measure of diligence, the sustaining excitement of becoming in the future some of what they are intended to be.

How we can intentionally attain personal and spiritual growth in the future in the light of what we decide to be in the present is the scope of this book.

All of us possess a future though it isn't for anyone to put a time clock or a crystal ball to it. We will use what time given to us, one way or the other, and each of us will either benefit by the proper use of that time, or we will allow it to pass with little or no creative advancement. In time, even quick change enthusiasts might become weary of their frantic endeavors and acquiesce to the tortoise philosophy that it is not how fast you run, but how soon you start and how steady you creep.

Nor is this a book on proper behavior. Who's to know? I only stress active participation in the simple process of doing small deeds over and over again, in the knowledge that these deeds hold in themselves the essence of all becoming. It is, as we practice the basic ABC's that we have a foundation on which to add the more sophisticated elements of learning. Small deeds, simply done, hold in them the quintessence of all great achievements.

I am overwhelmed with the preponderance of books in our libraries and bookstores dealing with improving our behavior, yet none has given, what I consider, satisfactory suggestions to the long haul of becoming a good person. The worthwhile books we do have are written chiefly to point up awareness and understanding. But understanding is not tantamount to good behavior and good behavior is not possible without the seeds of goodness planted in it. What makes proper or acceptable behavior is, as far as I am concerned, left to the judgment of the individual and is not the task at hand. This book cannot tell one what to be. I can only suggest, if one decides to become, the first step of that becoming is important and that continual practice is necessary.

One must be reminded that in the great works of art is found the fundamental elements of all good art. Shakespeare was not born a perfected writer. As a child, no teacher sat him down and ordered him to "write." If he was a good teacher he taught him how to fashion a letter one at a time often taking and guiding his hand but in all cases encouraging the small that would grow into the large and be held together by an ultimate performance. Bach was not commissioned to compose his masterpieces early. He was shown a clavier and a stool built high with pillows and taught the tedious scales. Likewise, Rembrandt was not the great artist at a tender age that we know today. He too had to dabble, as it were, with crayons before he could mix the oils into a blend of colors that produced the famous Night Watch.

Proper behavior, then, is subordinate to "experience." What a person does is only important in the light of what it adds to experience. Experiences can be remembered, evaluated and accumulated. We want our experiences to count.

As a new becomer myself, I now have some principles of becoming that I have hacked out of my own experience. Would that I had had someone, years back, do this job for me when first I began thinking about living with a purpose. The individual principles are not new. Nor have they been hidden; they have merely been overlooked or forgotten. I have sought to formulate a system of working principles of becoming that might prove helpful to others who also have a yen to become.

A principle has a certain operational condition that allows that principle to work. The principle of air conditioning does one little good unless all the doors of the house are closed. Similarly, our heating system would soon be on the fritz if we opened up all the windows. No system of heating, save the energy of the sun, can heat up the whole outdoors. Principles have specific conditions.

If one wants to become, one must set up the proper conditions that allow the principle to hold together.

Early in my thinking about becoming, a friend recommended Nathaniel Hawthorne's classic story—The Great Stone Face. I went to my suburban library and checked out the book, then searched out an old copy of my own. I thought I had read the story as a child but discovered it was, like many things, an event of the past that had been lost in the attic of my mind.

As I read the story, a childlike fancy came to me, a vision of one becoming, imperceptibly yet irrepressibly. The story is a simple one cast in the White Mountains of New Hampshire. Ernest, the hero, was a young boy living in constant view of a mountain that reflected to all the world the face of man, an image that bore confidence, serenity, stalwartness, compassion, understanding and grace. The face became the young man's daily companion and through the years the youth learned from the face the deeper truths of living. To make the story warm and believable the author weaves a legend into its fabric. Someday a man would come to the valley bearing the likeness of the Great Stone Face.

From time to time, a great man would appear; once an illustrious statesman, once a wealthy industrialist, a famous soldier, each hoping he would be the one whose likeness most resembled the face on the mountain. None qualified and the villagers were beginning to believe the tale was only in their imaginations and would never come true. As many would have guessed the ending, Ernest grew, through the years, to become the village patriarch, a man unpretentious but noble, humble and self-effacing. One day, in the twilight of the fading glow of the sun the young man, now old and wise, stood to preach. As he did the rays of the sun caught the old man's profile and cast it across the chasm onto the mountain. In a breath of utter amazement the sun revealed that the sage old man was indeed the likeness of the Great Stone Face. The young man became what he had most admired, what he had best loved and most revered. He became the face on the mountain.

Ernest was a becomer and we can learn from this beautiful story. What we most want to be can, indeed, be fulfilled in our lifetime. It may well be our only chance of truly becoming and quietly achieving the real turn-key person.

To be today what we want to become tomorrow is the simplest formula for growth I know and the idea holds subtle dynamics: quiet perseverance, gentleness and modesty. And I find it so compelling, so alluring that it projects one into a new process of experiencing. It gives one the clearest hope of attaining the full range of becoming, while at the same time involved in being on a daily basis. Yeats catches the tandem spirit.

O body swayed to music, O brightening glance
How can we know the dancer from the dance?

What the author left out of the story of the Great Stone Face is what I intend to add to mine. Becoming is not easily defined nor broken down into specifics. Hawthorne didn't go into detail of Ernest's becoming like the mountain. He didn't chart the progress or define the terms. He merely set the goal.

I do not think the art of becoming need be vague. As a way of life it can be brought down to explicit terms. We can name, define and develop specifics, not necessarily as admonitions faulting anyone's present life, but as suggestions that can begin, for anyone, the process toward a fuller life. I choose to treat the art of becoming, not as a craft, but as a purpose. Purpose here is used as a noun as well as a verb. "Daniel purposed in his heart...for his purpose was to worship God." The ultimate intent that moves a person to go out of his way and make an effort is a purpose planted in his heart. The art of becoming is that purpose. My intent is to offer guidelines, inspiration, motivation and some sensible rationale to make becoming a life-long and fulfilling purpose.

Little is found in school curriculum or in church catechisms that give instructions to the principles of purpose. Less is given to the formal education of values. Honesty is hoped for, integrity is admired, yet like gratitude and generosity, they are left to the house chores of the inner circle of the family. No one hears of a person taking a night course in patience, or of an extended education course in the art of discernment. We don't send our children to school to learn the techniques of kindness. We leave that sadly to the school of hard knocks. Therefore, I feel we have ignored the long range areas of soft data value education in favor of an education that packs the brains with the hard data of facts and figures. We, as a people, are bereft of a value system education based on a standard of personality development for wholeness and it leaves us content to live as incomplete beings.

The current affairs of our world headline the lack of such universal training and sensitive understanding among all classes, from the elite and powerful to the lowly and powerless. An obvious lack of patience is found in the statistic that in our country some estimate over 2,500 children under the age of five are killed or maimed each year by abusive parents. The obvious lack of integrity is shown in the open exposure of fraud, surveillance and cover-ups in high places. The obvious lack of generosity and the glaring abundance of greed are clearly measured in our rising crime rate and massive unemployment. The total disregard for the reverence for life ranges all the way from our plan to build nuclear weapons, anyone of which could destroy several countries on the earth, down to the battered wife syndrome, attitude toward abortion, euthanasia and the tendency many social agencies have to apply patchwork repairs on the effects of broken commandments. The innate quality of goodness so strongly taught in all basic religions, is sadly out of style. The chance of it being restored is further diminished when the minds of individuals are not exposed with repeated intensity to results that come by its use. Goodness is displaced by a false expediency that does not bring good results.

We live by influences we don't understand. In the past few years the term "quality education" has been used by the courts, school administrators and political pundits. But what is quality education? Most of us belong to families, to work groups, to fraternity groups, to churches and to civic organizations. Are integrity, self-discipline or goodness found in these places? The most influential institution in the world today is the media. The god television and the goddess radio have a responsibility to the vulnerable public to bring fair reporting, accurate data and first class entertainment. Do they? Are the professionals, which often are the opinion-makers of our society, measuring up to their standards of excellence? Are our courts ruling judiciously for all the people, or do they maintain a private preference list while the rest of us stand in line for a hearing that never materializes? Is our country run by special interest groups and professional lobbyists, paid to represent special causes rather than the good for all? The studies I have been watching lately are concerned with the moral decay of our country and the questions must be asked. Is it true that our morals are breaking down, is it because we cannot legislate morality or because we cannot or will not teach morality with conviction and determination either in our schools or homes?

Indifference to the proper education of values is also evidenced in the sad lack of confidence we have in these values to make a difference either in the world at large or in our lives in particular. Most of us have a secret suspicion we cannot change. We question the gimmicks that make change seem easy, and rightly so. We question, if indeed, we can change, is the change for the better? Since most values and religious programs have been held under the double eye of doubt, as is any word of authority today, we tend to steer clear of having to make a personal judgment concerning them. Situational ethics has placed the old-fashioned attributes of love, kindness, honesty on the scales of human values and imbalanced them with a heavy thumb. Absolutes are out— compromise is in. Our generation has happily subjugated honesty in favor of affluence, love for people for the love for things and has come to accept and further endorse the twisted philosophy that kindness doesn't pay—shocking behavior and blatant rebellion does.

However, the seeming hopelessness of our society need not deter us from developing integrity and goodness ourselves, indeed, it should be a prime reason to hasten the process.

We shouldn't allow ourselves to become victims of hopelessness or prey for the 'they' factor in our society. We should become instead "an ingenious contrivance."

My contractor friend, Avery Mays, tells me in his building of high-rises and multistory buildings that the latent strength of some materials is what allows his buildings to rise up to higher and higher levels.

These spring board mechanisms are called "ingenious contrivances." As I understand it, these ingenious contrivances do two things: they allow for the potential of future design to be built, and secondly, they operate in a way that extends the potential of each separate member of the structure. Mays explains a pillar as an ingenious contrivance, of itself it is useless and never realizes its purpose or strength until a heavy dome is placed upon it. As a dome is set the pillar for the first time exhibits its latent strength and purpose in being.

In the same way some soils need the help of an ingenious contrivance in order to become suitable for construction to begin. In building One Main Place in Dallas the sub-soil was inadequate as a load bearing base for a tall skyscraper. A pad, some twelve feet in depth, was built to hold the building, but the pad itself did not arrive at its optimum potential until the building was completed at thirty-two stories.

To play the role of an ingenious contrivance in society is to alter the course of our seeming hopeless state. Individually we can direct our collective future to higher levels, then as the weight of social concerns bear upon us our latent strengths are exhibited and our potential is extended. In creative terms this is called the 'divine afflatus' when we use the strengths and gifts we did not know we have for good we did not know we could accomplish.

Half the people believe if people could be converted to goodness the massive social, political and economical problems that threaten to undo the world would be soon resolved. The other half believe if people are forced by law or weapon to act as they ordered, then good will come. Both ways have been dramatically attempted, neither has triumphed.

My approach is in the power of a single act, a simple deed, a solo performance over which I and I alone have control.

At a political rally a young woman asked the wife of a presidential candidate, "What can one person do?" The wife answered, "Let me put it this way, look at Madelyn O'Hare." Or better yet to persons like Gandhi or Mother Teresa. A far greater illustration is the enormous spread of Christianity—the work and heart of a single person.

The underlying hope of this book is for people, as individuals, to find the way to become kind, generous, selfless and loving in individual acts and in experiences of the moment. The person who can act kind to a spoiled child who is crying for a popsicle has the chance of acting kind to the drunk revolving, as he often does, in and out of our jails on a weekly basis. The person who can be patient when a rude driver cuts in front of him has the chance of being patient when a rude executive, pressured from the concerns of business, lashes out in anger. The goal is simply but firmly to point out the minimum in being so that the maximum of becoming has its fair chance.

I hope further to bear a social witness to the fact that the basic virtues can pay off in the most advanced societies; that kindness and love still have a valid and needed place in our love of community; and that when we possess them the world's face is smiling. Socially, our chance of mutual survival rests on our personal becoming in order to meet the needs of the world around us. As we become good our goodness makes a difference in the lives of other people, else the task, much less the accomplishment is futile. But even if the result is minimal the act, nevertheless, is contagious. When we become good, not for the sake of goodness alone, but for the sake of the overall quality of life, we experienced, for the moment, being a world citizen with a cosmic love for all nature embracing the beliefs of dignity and cooperation.

Our country was founded on the principle of cooperation. Even before our founding fathers hacked out the Declaration of Independence the earlier settlers formed, in 1620, what was called the Mayflower Compact. This compact was a covenant—a covenant among the people striving for survival in a new land. It stated that all would agree voluntarily to subordinate their rival self-interest to the "general good of the colony."

James Michener in his book on the Quality of Live talks about his own immediate environment. The reason he enjoys living where he does is because he enjoys seeing deer browsing in the fields often early in the mornings. He says he is quite prepared for the fact that within a few years the pressure of population will force the deer to move on, out of his area. He adds, "I can accept the disappearance of the deer from my front lawn, but if they disappear altogether, as many species might if natural living areas are not preserved, I should experience a loss so great that I am not sure I would want to go on living in a world that has sacrificed so much. A good society does not require that the deer live on my lawn, but it does require that they live somewhere.

This planet, devoid of its natural inhabitants—animals and birds and fish and trees and flowers--would be desolation. It is quite possible that men require dogs and deer to keep them human.

It is also possible that we need cleaner air and quieter cities to keep us sane. There is a balance between beauty and business that must not be ignored.

The quality of a good life depends in large measure on how a man reacts to his natural environment, and we cannot destroy one without diminishing the other."

If we could start the becoming process in one individual heart and in one corporate community toward the reverence for all of life, we could gradually change the world. If one, then maybe it could become a common practice?

The government does it on a grand scale when it supplements hurricane Katrina's refuges from New Orleans; the church does it on a slightly lesser scale by providing shoes for children in Africa. We do it at home when we cut the meat equitably among our family or better yet cook a meatless meal once a week voluntarily as they do today in Russia on command. If our sensitivities are strong enough we may be like a friend of mine who, by actual count, took fifty-six ants out of his house and deposited them outside as an act of reverence for life. The becomer is one who becomes for reasons, large or small, and for the satisfaction of making the world a better place in which to breathe and move and survive.

I hope as you read on you will find suggestions that will catch fire and turn the tide on hopelessness, discouragement and futility. "Someday," wrote de Chardin, "when man has conquered the wind, the waves, the tide and gravity, man will harness for God the energy of love and then for the second time in the history of the world, man will have discovered fire." To give up on the world is to give up on ourselves and that is not a natural instinct of creation. This can be a good world when it is populated by good, generous, kind and sensitive people.

I offer this concept of becoming by being as a possible untried concept. Other alternatives have been explored with little results. Maybe activating a slow, deliberate, consistent means of changing the way we think and act, we can begin to change the world, if only a little bit at a time.

How? The mechanics for becoming by being are not machine made. Would that we could put ourselves through the rollers of a machine and print out, as might a computer, the perfect person who could neither be stapled or spindled. The production of becoming is far less sophisticated, but much more involved. The refinements have not been made. The wrinkles have not been ironed out. Becoming is open-ended and loosely defined. We cannot measure it by scoring points as we do in a football game; or chart it as we do sales; or explain it as we might a difficult quantum theory. The thing we can do is recognize it. And with the energies of the universe rough hew it and let the process shape its ends. Much like the wind it defies human capture and control.

As we discern the finer points of becoming it is easier to recognize. With clearer perception comes appreciation and when we actively appreciate the art of becoming for its own sake, we venture after it as one hungry to learn and know.

Our criterion for judgment is not productivity. We have been inundated with productivity and to my way of thinking concentration on productivity diminishes the potential toward creative becoming. The aim is simple sincerity. Then persistence, ingenuity and perseverance—become the key traits that move us toward excellence in being beyond whatever stage we find ourselves.

My design in becoming is not necessarily toward change for change's sake, though surely change will ultimately take place. I am not interested in substituting one thing for another like a vice for a virtue, though that too may conceivably happen. I am far more interested in adding on, in taking me as I am, and you as you are and building on our foundation of personal commitment.

Secondly, I am not interested in our becoming something tangible: a do-it-yourself auto machine, a sportscaster or a hockey player. I, rather, have in mind finding out if we can become deeper, broader and better by becoming diligent, disciplined and dedicated to who we believe we are and can be in our finest state of being. I want for us the qualities that make for greatness whether we have greatness within us or not. I know without the qualities of greatness there is neither the chance nor the hope for greatness.

These qualities can be found in many modern lives. Candice Jordan tells about her efforts to save the lives of hundreds of Biafra children. Back in the late 60's, Candice heard a news report on television that completely shattered her. Scenes of children starving because of the war in Biafra brought a terrifying fear to her. As she looked upon her own children she wondered if her home town was cut off from food supplies, due to war, would someone overseas be interested in feeding her children? The thought haunted her and within a week she took the train from her home in Westport, Connecticut to New York and sought out a charitable organization whose purpose was to help the world's children. She was told they were very much interested in the terrible situation and had sent a representative over and they should have some news back in October. "October!" she said. "This is June. Ten thousand babies might be dead by then." She asked what she could do now. They suggested organizing a small group in her own community and raise money for an airlift of food. Candice asked how she might start and called UNICEF (The United Nations' Children's Fund) and they in turn referred her to their Nigeria-Biafra information desk where she began to get some help. From that contact, Candice, with the help of her husband and many volunteers created Americans for Children's Relief.

From there the food ball started rolling. In a very short time Candice was on the Ivory Coast setting up a medical survey before repatriating the children. She said, "When I walked into the first camp run by the Red Cross and supported by the Americans for Children's Relief and the French Order of Malta, I was overwhelmed with joy as children surrounded me."

Candice Jordan's story is a typical one of becomers. She admitted she was caught up with an idea that possessed her. She said, "All of a sudden I was in a frenzy to do something. If I had thought at that moment that there were 300,000 children who needed help, I might have done nothing, but I wanted to do something to save the life of even one child."

Candice Jordan caught the spirit of what one person, one step at a time, can do and it all began with listening to a TV program, then taking the first train trip into New York City to check it out. This act changed the life and the direction of one Candice Jordan. Can you imagine how many childrens' lives it changed in Biafra?

The reservoir of becoming by being is full and as far as I know the supply will last forever. As long as time is measurable becoming will be possible. The process is also multi-dimensional. When I think of progress I see a flow chart that moves with a graph line diagonally up the page. Becoming has an upward tendency. However, we decide to utilize the thoughts and suggestions in this book, the direction can only be out and in and up and forward.

I think of becoming personally in a forward direction, but I think of becoming spiritually in an upward direction. I think of becoming generous in an outward direction. I think of becoming perceptive in an inner direction.

In the pathway of becoming will be spotted the specific deeds of being. Whatever the ultimate is for each of us, none can ever begin to attain until the decision has been made to venture the first step on that course. Advancement follows with each further step. We may enjoy periods of 'giant steps' but even they must be taken with purpose and planning. We may have to be satisfied with small accomplishment until we have enough experience to risk larger ones. We may have to govern our time and be content with slow progress even when we attempt daily deeds. Neither the rate nor the pace should trouble us. We don't measure our progress by anyone else's. We maintain our own counsel; yet, I dare say, that whatever it is we decide to become, in due time the world will know. Becomers are hard to hide for their steps always lead somewhere

START WHERE YOU STAND

If wishes were horses, beggars would ride. Theoretically speaking, becoming by being carries one beyond the third grade level of "wishing makes it so" and gives us some concrete underpinnings that more appropriately connect our thoughts with our actions. When I first proposed this idea to a friend, her response was immediate: "I'm not so much concerned about that the fact I need to change," she said, "I'm interested in the end result."

A measured assurance is what we all want. If one trudges the 898 steps up the Washington Monument, one wants to be assured, once up there, he can see all of Washington, a cloudy day not withstanding. Does the theory justify the energy it takes to support it? Does the cost of personal involvement pay off even if the process is slow and the progress inconsistent? Does it work?

A theory is much like taking the old horse to the pond: you can get him there, but you can't make him drink. The effort is worthless unless it's workable. The concept of becoming by being can be clearly workable if one builds on his understanding of the theory. It is theory within a theory as a box nests within a box.

All of us are becoming something. This is a theory. That each of us might become something intentionally by the practice of being intentional is another theory and that's the theory I am putting forth. As we are being, we can become, we can grow and we can enlarge our span of being that practice and time will help complete.

If the theory is valid it moves as does an idea into the main stream of one's being. It becomes a dynamic power flowing into the voids and vacuums of those committed to it. The idea has energy of itself, impulses and tendencies to exalt human nature, to magnify it and develop it.

Practically speaking, becoming by being is the process of becoming while one is experience being. Said another way, it is practicing what you want to become by acting as if you have already become. John Powell says, "The fully human person is an Actor, not a Reactor." He illustrates this in his story about the syndicated columnist Sydney Harris, accompanying his friends to a newsstand. The friend greeted the newsman very courteously, but in return received discourteous service. Accepting the newspaper which was shoved rudely in his direction, the friend of Harris politely smiled and wished the newsman a nice weekend. As the two friends walked on down the street the columnist asked: "Does he always treat you so rudely?" "Yes, unfortunately, he does," "Why are you so polite and friendly to him?" "Because I don't want him to decide how I'm going to act." Powell makes the suggestion that the "fully human person is his own person," and that he doesn't bend to every wind which blows, that he is not at the mercy of all the pettiness, the meanness, the impatience and anger of others. Attitudes do not transform him as much as his responses transform them.

By acting with kindness in an unkind circumstance or when kindness is not called for is becoming by being. This good friend of Harris' had learned to be kind by being the Actor under tough type of circumstances. Not only did he refuse to allow another to dictate his mood or his feelings, he worked the work of becoming kind by returning a kind gesture in response to a nasty dig. He acted kindly until by habit and ultimately by nature, he was innately kind, for as he admitted, he was always kind to the rude and uncouth newsstand man.

To come to the point in one's life when we can anticipate our actions in given situations is also the work of becoming. Soren Kierkegaard says, "Life can only be understood backwards, but it must be lived forward." How many of us lament, after we have finished a big piece of chocolate pie, "I wish I hadn't eaten that, I really didn't need it?" Well, most of us. We only see the salient truth of gluttony after we have gorged ourselves with the fattening delight. When we can look at piece of pie and say, "I don't need it, thus I won't eat it," we have progressed and turned the tables on a damaging compulsion. Instead of understanding backward, we understand and formulate our habits in a future direction.

Paul Tournier, the famed psychiatrist, encourages the idea of habit, he says, "Everything is habit in biology, and habits are created only by means of repetition. Experiments have shown how much our behavior is determined by the mental images to which our minds are constantly returning." By practicing over and over again we finally internalize our habit as an integral part of our make-up. Until then, we merely act as if we did have it.

Cast in a psychological framework, becoming by being might be called self-fulfilled prophecy. What we think about being, visualizing in our mind's eye or even fantasize, is, in time, actually fulfilled. Think of a person, for instance, who really desires to be generous. He doesn't say to himself, "Okay, from now on I am going to be generous." It doesn't work that way. For, in truth, we can't dictate our behavior that casually and expect noble and permanent results. What does he do? If he is sincere about the desire to be generous, he can first be generous with small amounts of money, realizing that a penny is the stuff of which a thousand dollars is made. I am reminded of what a great Quaker fund-raiser once said. "It is well to encourage the small giver, for if he is treated properly his interest will grow and he will become a big giver."

My husband becomes a fund-raiser in the fall of every year and he often points out how ridiculous it is of those who say they would give if they had the money. His theory is that if you don't give when your means are small, you surely won't give when you have plenty.

When we accept the concept of doing small things that leads to larger our theory broadens with future dimensions and becoming by being is viewed as visionary. Visionary, first as pictures in the mind and then as pictures that form a real possibility.

The vision then becomes the goal. Rarely does anyone day-dream himself to be less than perfect when he is thinking about himself. If I picture myself generous, I would never be a token giver. I'd be a Rockefeller. In a book on the lives of the Rockefeller family I took note of their giving history. Their giving didn't start with a million. It started when John D's had his first job as an office boy making $3.50 a week. The boy rigorously set aside thirty-five cents for the church or charity and when his income was close to 3.5 million a week, he carefully donated $350,000 of it to religious or humanitarian purposes. One doesn't have to be rich to be generous. Being generous can mean being generous with one's time, one's energy, one's concern or one's possessions. A generous speaker, for instance, is one who arrives at his engagement early enough to keep his hosts from having anxious moments. A generous church member is one who gets up early, dresses, picks up the mini-bus at the church and then rounds up the senior citizens and brings them to an occasion they would miss otherwise. A generous gardener is one who readily shares slips and cuttings from his flowers and plants with his neighbors. Corinne Updegraff Wells says, "You don't have to be rich to be generous, but most of us are rich in the possessions which make generosity possible. If one has the spirit of true generosity a pauper can give like a prince.

These so-called visions become clear to us as goals when we can identify them and call them by name. Benjamin Franklin went a step further. Not only did he establish goals and name them, he accounted for his success by writing a book of achievement. Franklin determined in his mind that if he was ever to achieve the success he desired he must first acquire specific talents. He then conceived goals within easy reach together with a definite plan to reach those goals. Each day he would check his progress toward the attainment of these goals. As he continued to focus his attention toward his goals he achieved each one of them.

Michelangelo once said, "In every block of marble I see a statue, as plainly as though it stood before me, shaped and perfect in attitude and action. I have only to hew away the rough walls that imprison the lovely apparition to reveal it to other eyes as mine see it." The becomers' eyes must learn to see goals as clearly as the great Michelangelo saw the finished figure before he picked up a chisel to make his first chip into the block of marble. One of the memorable lines in Sherman Edwards' play 1776 has John Adams saying as he stands alone in the Congressional Chambers in Philadelphia, "Doesn't anybody see what I see?" John Adams' saw and independent America and he set his goal.

I well remember someone complimenting my husband, "One thing about Gordon, he is always fair." Fair! I had never thought of fair being a virtue to be desired—you were either fair or not fair and that was that—like being right handed or left handed. I took a cutting glance at myself and realized I was one of those 'was nots' and began at that very moment thinking about becoming fair. I studied up on how to acquire fairness, and the first thing I discovered was—one needs a double set of everything. To be fair one needs two sets of senses; two sets of eyes; two sets of ears and feelings. I learned a person had to be objective and willing to look at all sides of a situation—even if through jaundiced or prejudiced eyes. I was to learn to hear what others hear, feel the pains they feel and walk in their soft moccasins.

I didn't want to buy our youngest son a new pair of tennis shoes. Admittedly, his were pretty worn and beat-up, but a new pair would look just like them in a matter of days. So when he asked for a new pair I stalled him. Later that week, our daughter came in asking for a pair of gold sandals. She didn't need them, but I wanted her to have them. Could I get them and be fair? Not really. I weighed my desire against my sense of fairness and took both small children to the shoe store.

When I was first stuck with the vision of fairness I realized its alienation to my natural character but I yearned for it anyway. I began to practice fairness at every opportunity and since that time fairness has served me well in my relationships and in my judgments. I learned not to be as opinionated. I learned to look with double vision. I learned to seek alternatives. After much time and many episodes of practicing fairness in small ways I have become infinitely fairer than I ever knew I could be. I think of fairness constantly. The process is not over. I have not reached 'fair heaven.' I have only caught the vision of fairness by permitting myself to be as fair as I know how to be deliberately. As a by-product, learning to be fair has made me appreciate when others practice fairness. I now recognize fairness and as I occasionally see it in myself, it is a self-fulfilled prophecy. Gerald Ensley points out that "excellence has an intrinsic attraction for men, whether it be of truth, or character, or beauty, or piety. We are made by our dreams of what life ought to be."

It seems to me, that it is how we see ourselves when trying to be and that picture provides the launching pad into becoming. This requires self-knowledge, a lively imagination and a whale of a lot of discipline.

But it all adds up to being real. For being real means that all our aspirations must fit sensibly and comfortably in the realm of our life goals.

Margery Williams has written a lovely book for children with an adult punch to it. The Velveteen Rabbit.

The story is about a stuffed rabbit that was found one Christmas morning in a young boy's stocking. The little rabbit wanted to become real and the writer tells the rabbit how to become real through the words of his friend, the Skin Horse.

"What is Real?" asked the Rabbit one day, when they were lying side by side near the nursery fender, before Nana came to tidy the room. "Does it mean having things that buzz inside you and a stick out handle?"

"Real isn't how you are made," said the Skin Horse. "It's a thing that happens to you. When a child loves you for a long, long time, not just to play with, but REALLY loves you, then you become Real."

"Does it hurt?" asked the Rabbit.

"Sometimes," said the Skin Horse, for he was always truthful. "When you are Real you don't mind being hurt."

"Does it happen all at once, like being wound up," he asked, "or bit by bit?"

"It doesn't happen all at once," said the Skin Horse. "You really become. It takes a long time. That's why it doesn't often happen to people who break easily, or have sharp edges, or who have to be carefully kept. Generally, by the time you are Real, most of your hair has been loved off, and your eyes drop out and you're loose in the joints and very shabby. But these things don't matter at all because once you are Real you can't be ugly."

These words belong on the shelves of the wise and the growing people of all ages. The distance between what we are and what we want to become is the gulf we swim and the deal is to make the experience of being the bridge that narrows the channel toward becoming.

How do we get there from here?

The other day a friend called, "How do I get to your house?" After greeting him, I asked, "Where are You?"
"Well, I don't know. I'm down here at a service station on a corner." I answered him. "Hey, how can I tell you how to get here when I don't know where you are?"

The shortest distance between two points begins when the two points are clearly identified. Where are we and where do we want to be? Maps are made to answer this question if we travel by car, bus or air to distant places. The modern Mapsco narrows the search within any city in our county. Floor plans direct us around our houses and offices and closet dividers and organizers complete the job. There are aids to help us locate ourselves on an invisible map but where are not maps that help us find ourselves? We must do this on our own.

My friend down at the service station had to find his bearings. He had to look around and gain some knowledge of his surroundings by locating a street sign or a landmark. When he did, I could then offer him detailed directions to my home.

As we look around, we might discover we are lonely and want new friends; we are a spendthrift and desire frugality; we vacillate and long for stability. Some of us may be impatient and purpose to be patient; others may have the desire to be honest when dishonest has long been a habit. There may be some who want to enjoy some peace of mind when all they have known is frustration and distraction. Some of us may simply want to become better organizers, more consistent performers, or simply more content.

Jean Nidetch, founder of Weight Watchers, faced a situation of a similar yet different nature in her life. Hers was physical. She was fat and wanted to be thin. She writes in her book, "Something has to make you very angry or ashamed enough to be able to say, 'Okay, help me.' I felt I was too intelligent to have somebody teach me how to eat, and in 1961 you didn't tell anybody that you were going somewhere to be taught what to eat and when to eat it. I knew that a green pepper was better than a cupcake. But there had to be a miracle that was going to make me look at a cupcake and say, 'I hate it!' And that was what I was looking for, a miracle.

A miracle, that blinding, once in a lifetime stunning event, that changes people overnight into what they need to become, rarely happens. Not that miracles don't happen or that the Divine Power can't perform them. It is just that God hasn't, and most likely will not send a lightning bolt to instantly transform the majority of us.

But conversion, which means to turn around, does not always have to stem from divine intervention. A person can change immediately and radically by his own will and self-commitment. A friend of mine learned from his doctor that to take another drink would shorten his life. That was the last day he ever took a drink. He didn't taper off, he stopped that day. When it dawned on our daughter the difference between how her nubbed-off finger nails looked and those of her friends she stopped biting her nails over night. One can make personal commitments fostered by a number of situations or religious experiences which, when they take place, alter the point of view of a person. Or one can be made aware of a bad habit that is no longer acceptable by family or society and that awareness becomes a stimulus for change.

When our son received and had to come up with the money to pay his third speeding ticket and then his insurance doubled he was forced to look at his foolish driving habits. Now he is nonaggressive driver. Whether the awareness is instant or by degrees, either way, the awareness prepares one for growth and change is forth-coming.

Jean Nidetch found, to her profitable amazement, that it really didn't take a miracle to lose weight. She lost weight by an alternate means. She formed a plan, supported by a desire and a determination to become thin.

A few years ago my husband became over weight and with a certain mental build up came to himself and said, "Enough is enough!" He went to Weight Watchers. In three and half months he was down to his normal weight. Those three and half months turned around our thinking about dieting. Weight Watchers proved first that dieting was strictly in the mind, or as Charlie Shedd said, "in the head." My husband was actually eating more than he had previously but it was regulated and selected. The food was now nutritionally sound, thus better for him. Secondly, once he had made up his mind to diet, the process was relatively simple. He placed his desires, not only in the realm of possibility, but in specific ounces and pounds. He knew what he wanted to become. He and others like him had a single goal. Weight Watchers took fat people and help them become thin and he wanted to be one of those people.

Another organization that struck me with their successful consistency in dealing with goal setting is Alcoholics Anonymous. This amazing organization has done more to rearrange lives and give people new directions than any organization outside the church. Their program, called Twelve Steps, is the principle of taking a person, devastated by the habitual use of alcohol, and helping him regain self-respect by becoming sober. The program begins with the initial admission of dependence and proceeds to a victorious liberation from the clutches of alcohol—one step at a time. Alcoholic Anonymous takes those addicted to drinking and drugs, then helps them return to society as sober, useful citizens.

In both these programs the transformation is real and it is clearly this type of progress I want to see in my own personal life, not necessarily a sudden change, but a realistic approach to becoming more of what I know I can be in specifics. I want the results to show, if not in a visible way, but in a noticeable, gradual, life-changing way. To become patient may not be seen on the surface, but it was a great day when my husband announced, after I had been privately working toward patience, "You know, I haven't seen you angry in months."

That's becoming.

Therefore, I believe that the theory of both Weight Watchers and Alcoholics Anonymous is sound. Inherent in their teachings is the emphasis of day-by-day achievement. Alcoholics Anonymous asks a person only to abstain from drinking just one day at a time. Weight Watchers encourage their clients to set a goal and they are rewarded for the loss of a single pound.

There is yet one more method, the practice of becoming by being.

When John Wesley, the father of Methodism, became confused by his own inner struggles toward becoming a faithful minister of the gospel, he confessed his so-called lack of faith to his friend Peter Bohler. Mr. Bohler admonished him: "Preach the faith until you have it, then because you have it, preach it." Peter Bohler, the Moravian preacher, intuitively felt that each of us has areas that need developing. He felt Wesley would not, in any way, be hypocritical to act his faith until he possessed it. In fact, he encouraged him and pointed out the process as a necessary first step toward finding his faith.

In all experimentation, including spiritual experimentation, there is the necessity of taking the hypothesis and holding it long enough to test its validity by "acting as if" it were true until it is proven by experience to be true or false. This is the practical approach to faith that has been literally a godsend to many people. Nobody ever learned to swim except by jumping into the water and acting as if he could swim. Nobody can learn to ride a bicycle, or play tennis, or speak in public or write a poem, until he acts as if he can do these things. When Pascal saw the truth of learning by doing, he commented, "If a man of goodwill expresses in practice the deeds and gestures which normally proceed from religious experience, there is opened to him a channel for the grace of God. There is thus provided a bridge…supplying a continuity otherwise lacking."

We practice, then, until the act becomes so much a part of us that we do it without thinking, automatically and instinctively. It soon becomes a spontaneous, normal response and in time becomes an integrated part of our make-up. Phillips Brooks said, "Routine is a terrible master, but she is a servant who we can hardly do without." Whether we like it or not, most of our learning is by rote and routine that evolves finally into some sort of ritual or regiment, and we know from experience that everything improves with exercise, be it a practical performance or a spiritual discipline.

One evening an intense young man sat on the edge of the couch in our living room expressing, with convincing emotion, his jolting intentions.

"I'll fake it! If that is what it takes to keep my marriage, I'll fake it. I'll be the most religious person you ever saw."

Bill and Janet were having premarital counseling with my husband and me. In just four weeks they were to be married and had come to the house to discuss a crucial difference in their religious outlook.

They were wise in dealing with the problem early. Janet held strong religious convictions. She felt the need for regular church attendance and an active prayer life. She expressed a hope that the two of them might have some mutual spiritual grounds on which to base their marriage. Bill had no desire to make a habit of going to church, yet he believed in God and professed a religion 'within himself,' which excluded what he called the institutional church. He felt his type of religion was fully sufficient, and he definitely did not want her cramming her religion down his throat.

As the evening wore on Bill discovered that the probability of happiness in his future marriage might well stand or fall on his support of his wife for the church. He blurted out that if it came to that he would honestly be dishonest about religion, or at least, his need for it. He'd fake it.

I couldn't help but reinforce him. "Try it," I said, "if that is all you have at the moment, use it."

To fake anything may startle the pious-minded who believe that motives should be pure and honest and unquestionable in all ways. Yet we must be careful and not let the word 'fake' trip us up. We are all fakers. Who of us has never bluffed to get our way or smiled to a friend and pretended the remark just made went straight through both ears when, in fact, it punctured the pit of our stomach? Who of us has never feigned conviviality when bored stiff or eaten two pieces of Aunt Lois' rhubarb pie just to please? Testing our own behavior we clearly see our fakeness, our shams and false faces, and we might gain a bit of sympathy for the young man.

You see, Bill was declaring himself to be an honest pretender. He was saying, I am going to practice, to improvise, to play (as in music) without script or score in order to try to produce harmony. He was not faking to deceive, but was honestly attempting to bridge the church-gap between them. He would fake being what Janet wanted him to be, until the acting made him, in truth, what he pretended to be in the first place.

This, then, in its deepest sense, is a spiritual exercise. To pretend goodness is what C. S. Lewis calls "dressing up like Christ." To practice being what we want most to be is the only learning process we know. It is putting into action convictions of the mind, uniting the physical act with a spiritual value and thus operating with integrity.

Each insight helps us accept what and who we are physically, emotionally and intellectually. It is essential to know who we are as completely as possible in order to learn more about our potential and become convinced we are on the right track. We must, however, be realistic about our limitations. We must be careful, however, to look past our dreams and our periodic moments of self-indulgence, convincing ourselves we are something we are not. We begin in the only way we know. We listen, test and explore who we actually are, and with each day by experiencing our true self be rejuvenating. We are forever changing, always becoming a new person, always involved in the constant process of re-creating our own personality. We trust in our abilities and resources, confident that we can adapt to and cope with all the challenges that life will present, and then rise to the occasion of ultimate becoming.

No one can direct our feet. No one will take us by the hand and guide us, as they once did when we were children. Now that we have grown tall we are to put away childish excuses and get to the business of fully being. The prospects in store are housed in the hours ahead but one starts with the thought that now is the earliest opportunity.

IT'S A PROCESS

The function of process is as evident as the morning newspaper, yet it's as chimerical as a desert mirage. We know about the process of printing that newspaper, or the process of making a fudge cake, or even the process of electing our governmental officials upward to the national level, but the word and meaning of process defies all systems we have of defining it. Process is like breathing, it's simply something we do, unconsciously and continually. Process is a faceless, shapeless phenomenon. We can't feel it, touch it, or smell it. We can't weight it on a scale, measure it with a yardstick, or tabulate it on a calculator. There is no question; process is an elusive abstraction with no credentials. Yet, we know for certain, process if factual. It is a silent procedure that quietly links step by step many elements into a whole.

In a notable television commercial years back the selling line is, "Wonder Bread helps build strong bodies eight ways." As the narrator explains the product, the camera, through trick photography, allows the viewers to see a child, in rapid sequence, grow from babyhood to adulthood. What our eyes see, like physical growth, we say we understand whether we definitely understand it or not. We also understand the word and concept of becoming— when becoming is becoming 'something.' The way our society is these days we all must become something.

One afternoon when our daughter was in college we were visiting her. As we were sitting in the Student Union Building having a Coke, one of her friends walked up and joined us. After a bit, I asked this new friend what her father did for a living. Before I realized it I also asked, "And what does your mother do?" Later, I was shocked by the fact that I would feel it important to ask such questions. As parents we are guilty of classifying. We are interested in what a person does, so that we can more quickly determine who a person is. Our society, productively oriented as it is, is ready to assemble, box and market us, male and female, according to what we can do. When we ask a person what he does for a living we instantly know 98 percent of all we need to know about that person. If he is a banker, or she's a real estate executive we know where they live, where they buy their clothes, where they spend vacations and where the children go to school. If she is a cleaning woman or he is a garbage collector we know the same information, although the information will be different. Work is the only identifying ethic we understand and we understand it in dollars and cents.

As a youngster, if I worked hard and made good grades, learned a skill or passed a test, I was told I could become a lawyer or a librarian or whatever else I chose to be. The classic question asked of me was. "What do you want to be when you grow up?" Believe me, in my day when that question was asked few answered industrious, consistent, stalwart, frugal, or sincere. Heavens! The answers rang more like a siren and a train whistle toward firemen and engineers, airplane pilots and Hollywood movie stars. Characters in these categories were the only acceptable and honorable heroes we had. As we grew older our vocations and occupations took a more serious turn for we found we were praised according to our work ambitions. Everyone wanted to be a doctor, a lawyer, or a judge in the social milieu of our times. When my three children were preparing for their future, I admit to a certain amount of pride in saying one is in pre-med. This doesn't say I have more regard for one child over the other, but it does point out that pride in what a person becomes professionally carries enough social prestige that many aspirations are motivated accordingly.

All kinds of phony rationalizations would have to be invented if I had a daughter in school learning to be grateful, diligent or noble. These are after the fact qualities, certainly not her primary goal. They must take the back seat as side benefits we only hope come along with all the important training in becoming money makers.

The silent process of becoming, not a 'something,' but a complete being is the process that now interests me and I believe it's as much a part of the growth process as physical development. Had I had the push and prodding I received from my parents and friends to be patient that I had to become a school teacher I might now be able to better understand human relationships. Mindful always of this personal need to be patient, I was, nevertheless, denied any formal instruction on how to achieve it. There were no textbooks or manuals on patience learning in my school. The possibility of my becoming patient always seemed to be there but I missed a vital lesson on what to do to affect the machinery to get the process moving. What I did know was that simply applying 'x' marks on a calendar was not becoming. Becoming was not inherent in time—that when I was grown, or when I was older, or when I was educated I would then be all that I wanted or needed to be. Nothing of what I wanted to become was coming to me chronologically. I didn't grow generous as I grew tall, nor did I grow patient as I grew older, in fact I felt the opposite trend. As I grew older I was getting lazier, more intolerant and opinionated. Somewhere I felt I had missed a vital class.

As I thought of the graphic Wonder Bread commercial I realized the process of growth is readily accepted in the physical body. To accept process and growth as it builds one's personality and then is augmented into behavior is harder simply because it is not visual or openly apparent. A camera cannot take pictures of personal growth and scrapbooks are not kept in order to recall when we were babies in being as we were babies in the flesh.

Whether we can chart this process or not doesn't deny the fact that people are in 'soul' process.

Unbeknownst to us, while we are constantly experiencing the internal physiological processes of change, even to the level of cells multiplying and dividing within the body, we are subliminally changing our outlooks and attitudes. The chronicle of practical living floods us with stimuli from every area in which we are involved. Thus, as our being is in active process, our lives continually change. We are in movement and in constant flow of physical, psychological, intellectual, emotional and spiritual change from the time of conception. And as far as I know, this growth process is open-ended. Some believe that even the death event may be the birth of a new becoming sequel.

Erick Fromm comments that "there is simultaneously permanence and change in any living being; hence, there is permanence and change in any concept reflecting the experience of a living man." This is what living is, the tension between permanence and change as experienced personally from birth to death. As I looked for some means of casting this growth experience on a screen for the purpose of viewing I found it in the strangest place.

I was at a Press Club Seminar. A panel of distinguished guests was introduced: the mayor of the city, a state representative, the editor of the woman's section of the local newspaper, a TV commentator and a dean of a university. As a way of opening up the discussion the TV commentator asked the dean, "How do you teach integrity." The dean was obviously thrown a curve. She had been anticipating a media type question and fumbled the answer. Other members, equally unprepared, attempted to tackle the question, then, let it pass. Later on in the discussion the dean came back to the question since she was dissatisfied with her ambivalent answer, but she rambled on for several sentences without clarity or satisfaction. The word integrity caught me and I felt that if we really understood the meaning of the word, the answer would be forthcoming. The word integrity is interpreted in our society as operating with consistency, that is, to do and behave in a consistent way. This is true, if one understands that the word integrity also means wholeness, as does the word integration. The meaning is then clarified.

We can begin teaching integrity when we understand how to teach a person to become whole. As complex and complicated as this might sound, it merely means to view the person in a totality of mind, body and spirit. This, to me, then solidified my way of viewing the process of becoming. If I can understand wholeness I can more clearly understand the idea of becoming by being, and realize that the idea, in itself, has its own DNA complete with its own power and energy to pull us along.

As I am becoming whole and integrated, becoming begins to take place.
Wholeness is the sum of various and diverse parts. As each part is orchestrated and properly blended, as each element and attribute is fully utilized, wholeness is the result.

The simplest way to picture this is to reduce integrity of self down to its least common denominator. A person is an autonomous entity. He is an absolute. We might compare a person to a wall. A wall is a wall whether it is made of stone or wood or straw—but its potential is endless. Its function might be to keep in water, keep out cattle, act as a snow barrier, or define a state line, an army barricade or a landmark. It might be high or low, ageless or temporary, sturdy or spindly. The wall might be white or green or brown. But it is still a wall. Being is like that. Clark Moustakes says, "being refers to this concrete holistic patterning of self in immediate living, as well as the unyielding, absolute and unique qualities and...can be understood only in itself alone, as whole, not in terms of attributes. It is an individual unity...The individual self, or being is an ultimate core of reality which remains unchanged throughout changes of its qualities or state."

If we can see this—we can picture wholeness. Once we establish our being as (w)holistic, we then can add attributes. Attributes, however, do not add to the primary concept of wholeness. We can say, "There is a high, red brick wall." The high or the red brick does not make it a wall. It is a wall, both high and constructed of bricks, that

this time, happens to be red. I am me—regardless of the hundreds of descriptive attributes and characteristics ascribed to me—I am me with possibilities of becoming, heavens know what!—wise, fair, genuine, peace-loving. But I am first—me.

Two factors bear then upon the process of being and becoming whole: creativity and time.

To be alive in being is expressed in being creatively involved in what goes on in our life. It means, we by nature, are acting upon and responding to all forms of experiences. If our reactions and responses are positive these experiences can become creative experiences. But, like a wall, we are an absolute. As we are involved in moving, changing, emerging—toward wholeness we then are creative. We add color, style, and dimensions that make us different from anyone else.

I believe creation is not finished, but constantly busy re-creating itself. From conception, continues Moustakes, (creation develops) as a continuous transition from one form to another. I believe we are doing the same. We are an entity but not a fixed entity. We participate in life, adjusting, conforming, adapting, while at the same time piloting progress in a creative way by being assertive and interested in self-expansion in order to influence our own fate. We make things new as does all creation by experiencing new things in the old and old things in the new.

An individual, who is in a creative process, is one who by-passes society's stereotypes. He is, rather, in the creative driver's seat, being himself. If he lives creatively he will not only be a part of the on-going process, he will be part of the production. Listening, for instance, can be either passive or active. I quote myself in a statement that has become an adage around our house. "One hears with his ears but listens with his mind." Being a creative listener means to hear and listen. One is passive, the other is purposefully active.

Michael Drury tells about her grade school experience when a teacher trooped the class out doors to lie down in the spring grass and make note of sounds they could hear. "We would call them out and she would write them down. An airplane overhead; boys shouting on the baseball diamond behind the school; the intermittent crack of hickory on horsehide; the splat of ball in a glove; a dog barking; cars shifting gears; birds in the acacia trees; wind in the acacia trees; wind in the willows, which was different; a screen door slamming in the house across the road; someone sawing wood; the phone ringing in the principal's office; wait—the murmur of insects in the grass around our ears."

As soon as we listened with purpose or for a reason a seemingly inactive verb takes on creativity. A few years back I wrote an article entitled, "Listening Can Stop Your Self-Consciousness." The idea of the article was to take the paralyzing trait of self-consciousness and with the tool of listening (a natural assignment for shy people), make that tool work for them. Turn the situation around and allow the art of listening to turn timidity into confidence. I offer three specific suggestions: listen to the words for their denotations, connotations and intent; listen with eyes to gain what the psychologist calls non-verbal communication or as Gibran said, "the voice behind the voice," and then listen in depth—fill the mind with the total sound of the total expression. I believe this is a prime factor leading to the success of stereo sound. It completely encases a person, surrounding him totally. When we apply these thoughts to listening we learn not to be afraid of silence. We find, if applied, no one need be tongue-tied and there is never any real reason to jump in with words to save an awkward situation.

If a person becomes a purposeful listener his experience will instill confidence in his role and soon dispel his feelings of self-consciousness and allow the person to become an active, equal partner in conversation. In this regard I agree with J. L. Moreno that creativity is a 'sleeping beauty.'

I caught a news item the other day. According to a French driving instructor, singing quietly to oneself, as one drives, is a great way to avoid accidents. As we know, driving can be dangerous. But this young instructor noted that in over ten years of driver's-ed teaching, her students had not a single automobile accident or received anything more serious than a parking ticket because they hummed while they drove. She insists, "Humming takes the tension out of traveling.

But listening creatively and driving creatively are two things we can start doing today. They are small ways we can begin to become patient, serene, stable. They also have in them the higher elements of grace—the stuff of which beauty is made.

Creativity, as a concept, came home to me when I gave up a long, held, tightly guarded hang-up. There was a time when I wouldn't allow anyone to read what I had written. Even today it affords me some embarrassment. I am aware it is a form of self-consciousness or pride, maybe fear or insecurity; but I suspected people of saying behind my back what they wouldn't say to my face if they thought my work—ordinary. Ordinary I couldn't stand, and it was not what I ever wanted to be. Ordinary and common were two words my mother never allowed me to use together with shut-up and stink. "Nothing that is worth anything is ordinary or common," she would say. To her, these words were almost blasphemy. But today, though I am not comfortable with people reading my words I have become, to a measure, receptive and open to it, bearing in mind the very process of reading words I put on paper is a process of my becoming less sensitive and more confident. If I stifled them, curbed them or subdued them I would be choking the life out of my own creation. For me to allow my written words to fall on the eyes and ears of others is one of the truly creative things I do. I realize only as I allow my words to be read can I creatively write and by the critical responses of those who read them become closer to what I want to become as a writer.

The second factor contributing to wholeness is time. Time is intrinsic in the process of becoming, says Harvey Potthoff. When "the individual is engaged in leading his life in the present, with a forward thrust into the future..." he is talking about becoming with its implications of change and transformation.

No one need prove himself; he is in being and while he is in this life he is cast in the limitations of time. When the principle of time is transcended, then the principles of being will be likewise. Until then, our beingness is in process as time as in motion.

I consider my being the most that I can be today a compelling force for my becoming what I shall become tomorrow. Only as I exercise my right to be today can I direct my becoming tomorrow. To be the most I can be at this moment is not only to be the architect of my future but the harbinger as well.

Many years ago I went back to college with the admonition that in five years I was going to be five years older anyway, I might as well have something to show for it. I lacked several hours for my initial degree, but the university's requirements specified that I should take thirty hours or one full year to fulfill residential requirements from the university granting the degree. This act, in fact, had a direct bearing on what I am today, not necessarily in an academic way or a vocational way, though that too was affected, but in a being way. I picked up an option and I became so involved and interested I continued all the way through the graduate program. Had I not made that choice I would have continued to drift through the days with nothing to show for it. Granted, had I merely drifted through the days, I would have also become—but the dynamics of being in action, involved in study, participating in thinking added enormously to my becoming that would not have been otherwise. Since I can see myself having achieved some measure of becoming in those years, I believe if I continue to creatively work at being, I will further become.

I think it is significant that the becoming direction might change or alter or even be replaced by another desire to become. Personally, I find that growth does this for me. Once I have a new thought or experience a new event my presupposed need to become this or that is often preempted and I regoal, so to speak. To be schooled, for instance, regoaled me; working with civic organizations regoaled me; and being closely involved in a political campaign regoaled me. Writing this book, has definitely regoaled me and I can say I am now a different person from whom I was when I first began to write about my continuous journey in becoming. Even as I write these lines the time and the becoming dots are adding up.

William Stringfellow, whom I admire for his theological insights once said, "I would be happy to die tonight." He felt that all he should be today was enough, but that if he was granted another day of another year he would live each day with the same attitude. I understand what he meant, but I find his thinking lacking a creative future. As I look back on my life and see what the years of personal training and education can do I must ask and anticipate what more time and more insights, more reading and learning can do for me. I would feel short changed if I were to die before I could become, yet I think, in all fairness to Stringfellow's philosophy, if I were not granted additional days or years I would be grateful for what I have indeed become to this moment. I suppose I am opting for the privilege of finding out what I can still do with my future. The fact that I now know more about myself, the world and the intent of creation only spurs me onward and upward for that which is yet for me to know and be. I have learned that I can only reach that higher state of being by earnestly, deliberately, consciously striving for it existentially in the here and now.

Time, therefore, mysterious as it is, has to be dealt with and the process of becoming leads me to enjoy the process of discovering being within the framework of time. We are all temporal creatures existing in a reality of a past, a present and some degree of a future and our destiny has to be directly related to this.

A friend of mind, interested in the concept of temporality lived out an ideal illustration of our being constantly reminded and beholden to the past. He was telling me about his experience in attending a Holy Week Service at the Antioch Baptist Church on Railroad Street in historic Bedford County, New York. What he felt brought to mind his place in time. The service was evangelical in nature. The choir and congregation sang old hymns such as 'Blessed Assurance," "Pass Me Not O Gentle Savior," and my friend felt he was back in his own past, remembering the revival meetings attended during his childhood in the southwest.

Much of what we are today is the product of layers and layers of experiences: some traditional, some radical, others traumatic, most of which have been long since forgotten as inconsequential. We can no more annul our past than we can sever ourselves from our bodies. But we can understand ourselves in some limited way when we gather up our backgrounds memories and past influences and see how they collectively work in and out of the present. Properly understood and properly interpreted the past can help us see ourselves in a truer light. Often this is the penetrating work of a psychotherapist or an analyst, the theory being that if one can evaluate and make mature assessments of the events of the past that knowledge may shed some light on one's behavior being acted out in the present.

To be a person in time is also to understand the self in the now; taking an honest inventory of ourselves as we perform our daily routines. Accepting the experiences of the past at all levels, then using them as arrows pointing us to where we are today.

For some people the present experiences are of utmost value, what is past is past and what can be looked for in the future is only a direct by-product of the present. Past or present hopes, revelations, liberation and untried experiments are simply not important. The fulfillment and consummation of life is not in the distance, but caught up totally in the now.

Children have this tendency of thought. The immediate is the only world they know and the only happiness they understand or can deal with. I have often felt Christmas is the one time to teach children about the future. Christmas is seeing, with all the excitement one can generate, an end in sight. Christmas always comes. And the waiting for it is always worth it.

There was a rule in our home as the children grew up about getting toys. Our children were typical children. What they wanted they wanted Johnny-on-the-spot. When they had allowance money of their own they couldn't see why they shouldn't get what they wanted immediately. We devised a "bird in the bush" plan that, I think, helped demonstrate to our children the value of time. When one of them would come and ask for a new toy we always said they could have it. "Give me your money," I said, "and I will put it on the mantle in the den and if, in two weeks, you still want the toy, you can buy it." Well, you know what generally happened. The money was spent many times on the mantle, but rarely at the stores.

If, indeed, the need was lasting, the toy was bought and time had made that toy more valuable and endearing.

Young people have a similar concept of their being in time. It's reflected in their dress, their life-styles and in the songs:

> I can't be contented with yesterday's glories,
>
> I can't live on promises, winter to spring.
>
> Today is my moment and now is my story, I'll
>
> Laugh and I'll cry and I'll sing.

There are other people who press with enthusiasm toward the future, living the All-American dream, a dream they couple with faith, as stressed in Christian doctrine, for a Christian is, by interpretation, a hopeful creature. The teachings of Christ bear out hope and speak of the future in vivid terms and exhort followers to lay up treasures for the future. Most of us believe there will be a tomorrow, but the Christian concept is that tomorrow can be better.

The future, of itself, cannot be fulfilling. The ingredients that make for personal fulfillment come from the ability, as well as the knowledge, that we can have some bearing on our own future. The future doesn't fulfill; we fulfill the future. We are co-creators, co-designers in fact, of the days ahead. This means, that our wills, choices and desires unite with the Source of all life to make our future different and hopefully better.

We are told that the acorn, if left alone, becomes a great oak tree. But I doubt this. It seems to me even an acorn needs the heat of the sun, the nurture of the soil and the water supplied by rain. If left alone, we may in the future become our intended creation, but I doubt it. We need to be spurred on, nurtured, fed and encouraged. The silent push each person feels within places us into the future and gives us the incentive to flesh out our own future Each one of us has had to accept certain facts, for instance, that our teeth aren't straight or our ears don't lay flat, or our knees are knobby, but all of us know, regardless of our outward development, our inner development, emotional or intellectual or spiritual, good as they are, can be potentially better.

The past, present and future seem clearly distinguishable segments in our lives, but I am proposing the idea of a new tense— one that is open-ended and not distinctively measured. The past is always behind us, the present only short lived and the future directly ahead, but the new tense, the tense of continuity and endurance develops in the protracted dimension of time. There is neither a starting point nor a duration point of the sustaining tense. It is not divided into day and night and hours and minutes, but in height and depth, length and breadth of the character of the becomer. In the Greek language there is what is called the aorist tense, which when used indicates that not only is something being done, it keeps on being done.

William Barclay tells a story about a small group of people in the Scottish Highlands. They were talking about heroism: they were saying that everybody, sooner or later, practices some heroism. A young man turned to an old woman; she looked so ordinary and uninvolved and was unaware that life had been for her a series of tragedies. "And what kind of heroism do you practice?"

he asked with an obvious air of thinking there could not be any kind of heroism in a life like hers. "I" she answered, "I practice the heroism of going on."

The time ahead, the now that makes the future, blooms from the seeds planted today—the seeds that cause the future to alter it course and cautions the future to give them sway. Time, then, becomes flexible—not fixed.

Harvey Potthoff, writing about the process of becoming a Whole Person in a Whole World, says that we human beings are a wonderful mixture of body and spirit and matter and mind, and we do not simply live in our bodies, we live our bodies. He continues, "That in the divine order, body and spirit, mind and matter are deeply interrelated and that we are thus born to be "whole" creatures."

When accepting one's emotional and intellectual self as matter of factly as we do, the process of our bodily growth involves coming to grips with a working relationship with the physical dimensions of our being. And this is the principle—the cardinal organizing principle undergirding process. Scientist are quick to note the process of growth with height attainment or size attainment or ultimate biological attainment—seeds though small grown to large trees—protoplasm into animals and babies into men—everything grows toward a pre-specified goal. But as Levi Olan once said, "From the first cell to Albert Einstein there is a long period of growth, billions of years. What is significant is that each stage is succeeded by a higher form." This places us in a process as part of the natural growth flow and we should acknowledge it in its totality.

Perhaps we can also agree that to place a person's achieving and aspiring tendencies in the stream of time is all together a different order of becoming and thus a higher challenge. We might also agree that the intangibles of mind and spirit, emotions and intellect can achieve in the divine order as the bodily maturation is witnessed in the physical order, making creative becoming functionally divine—ongoing, uplifting and fully (w)holistic.

The process goes on—and on—and on. And the excitement is in the sustaining knowledge that with each step, each forward motion, each modicum of achievement, the joy is in the process. Becoming is to being as the joy of planning a trip is to making one. Waiting for Christmas builds as each package gathers under the tree and the great morning only holds the excitement for the moment. Most of us enjoy aspiring as much as the achieving and both are of value in the process of becoming.

A NEW MIND SET

The same fire that melts the butter hardens the eggs. To really become, creatively and with satisfaction, the mind and the will (head coaches to action) must be activated—but activated in a new inventive way. For this, there is no clear formula. No one can tell another exactly what to do and no pattern can be universally drawn that fits every person. But it makes sense, if one is seeking personal growth through spiritual development and is not experiencing that growth, a new mind set is essential.

A quick examination will tell us if we are governed by our mind or by our body. Try this experiment. See the chair before you. Look at it closely. Look then at the clock. Now try to concentrate on that chair and that chair alone for ten minutes. To one who is not disciplined in the art of meditation, it is right-nigh impossible to keep one's mind on a single object. All kinds of thoughts dive in and out of our heads willy-nilly. Usually, one can't clear the mind for a single minute, the traffic is so thick. The truth is if our bodies were half as unresponsive to our wills as our minds are, we would never get out the front door or across the street safely. We simply do not have a firm grip on our minds. We cannot concentrate on a simple item for over a short period of time. We have much more control over our arms and legs, our lips and our kidneys than we do our minds. And yet, from our minds come the dictates of our being.

Our will is, likewise, fickle. What we purpose in our minds to do is not always what we do. The Apostle Paul lamented this fact; he said, "O wretched man that I am, who will deliver me? The things I want to do I don't seem to do, the things I don't want to do, I find myself doing."

We can all relate for this is clearly a universal statement. What is this internal chameleon that changes with every wind that blows? What causes inconsistency and this double mindedness? Why do we not operate in the balance of integrity? I offer three insights bearing on our see-saw behavior.

Growing up I was not a broccoli eater. In fact, I thought it tasted, smelled and looked like something dredged up from the bottom of the ocean. Now it is my favorite vegetable. How do we account for this?

While we were living in a small community outside of Dallas I decided to stop drinking coffee with sugar in it. Gradually, I weaned myself off of sugar by using less and less in each subsequent cup of coffee. Now, if anyone dips a spoon in my coffee cup that has stirred coffee with sugar or saccharin in it I can detect it instantly and all but spew it out of my mouth. Can this be explained?

We mature we say. What's mature about liking green broccoli and black coffee over green beans and sugared coffee? Our tastes change.

In order to properly illustrate the popular children's book, Make Way for Ducklings, Robert McCloskey lived with a handsome group of mallard ducks. They inhabited his studio in New York for weeks while he watched and sketched them. Since Boston was the scene of the book McCloskey's assignment was to tour Boston as one might tour it from the point of view of a duck. This brought McCloskey to his knees. And Boston never seemed so strange. From our vantage point of height Boston takes on entirely different dimensions and perspectives when seen from a duck's level.

We remember as children how tall our fathers seemed and how huge our Christmas trees were. From that time until this our perspectives have changed our points of view. As we have progressed from the duckling level we not only enlarged our vision, our steps are longer. We now move farther faster. But often in our race for speed we lose the particulars in the rush and tumble of life's traffic.

When I was born the world was 100,000 light years in diameter. Today it is 12 billion years in diameter. This fact alone is staggering evidence of the necessity to lift our eyes above the level of ducklings. Our world is larger, our responsibilities heavier, our options more plentiful. From every angle our viewpoints have altered.

As a writer I have studied how other writers graft their stories or their articles and the advice they give to young writers. The first writer will tell them to get the story down and then rewrite, rewrite and rewrite. The second writer will tell them to buckle their seat belts to their chair in front of the typewriter or computer and keep the pages rolling and eventually something will take shape, a theme, a plot, a personality—finally a novel. Writer number three will advise them to formulate a structure and then methodically follow it. A fourth will say write from notes and the fifth will suggest, especially if he writes mysteries, have the ending in mind before beginning the story.

All of these are legitimate writers and they are honest in their evaluation of writing for themselves and suggestions for others. Since, each writer has his own style and with his own method, I believe, without a question, most of them will caution any fledgling writer, "don't do it my way, try your own." There is no right way. Methods vary. And so do we.

Our wills cannot be nailed down. Nor would we want them to be, any more than we might want to review the situations and circumstances of the future. Take a poll of any ten friends and the likelihood of any of them wanting to know their future is rare. They may be curious but when it comes down to it, none would really be comfortable knowing what the future holds. If the future is uncertain and only limited predictions can be made about it, the will needs to be as flexible as the weather and as quick as a darting fly. What is this will then and how do we harness it without strangling it?

The power of the will or will-power has all but fallen in disrepute as a dirty word since most of us abuse it and are frustrated by it. We think we've got it when we don't and we don't have it when we need it. Our rationale concerning the will, therefore, needs constant review and testing.

Recently, Robert Assadioli, a pioneer psychotherapist, probed the will and discovered what to me is a hopeful thought to all becomers. He says, "on the cultural and scientific level the return of the will is due to the development of humanistic psychology that ignored many basic human subjects: love, joy, inspiration, intuition and will." He goes on to say that people are now becoming aware of their need for some higher regulation and control, some order and harmony, instead of chaos.

We need the capacity of the will to help us filter the basic attributes from that which is not worthy to that which is worthy.

I don't believe there can be any sudden refinement of the will, but I do believe there is sudden awareness or moments of excitement that comes over one, causing the will, if but temporarily, to see the possibility of something more. When this happens, the quickening of the inner life pushes us out of ourselves and into the future, and this brief sudden "enlightenment," if caught at the arc of receptivity, can start the process of becoming. If it is allowed to continue and maintain itself in sustained excitement, we become open to new possibilities that lead to potential fulfillment.

Some call this the A-HA experience.

That is why through the art of becoming I am stressing a fresh look at the will, maybe from a new angle, possibly from a different side. Paul Tournier, in his book The Person Reborn, tells about a poster he once saw in an Italian railway station. The poster was advertising some product under the name, 'Cervin.' The picture on the poster represented the Matterhorn, which as a French speaking Swiss, Tournier had known as Mont Cervin. The picture attracted his attention because there was something odd about it. He soon discovered what it was: it was the Matterhorn seen from the Italian side, with its peak pointing to the right. As a Swiss, Tournier was used to seeing the Matterhorn with its peak pointing toward the left. He said, "You cannot view the Matterhorn from the Italian side and from the Swiss side at the same time. Nevertheless, it is still the same mountain."

There are many sides to every person, every issue, every subject and there are equally as many ways of viewing them. No clear pattern surfaces for a person to flesh out his potential; yet Rene Dubos insists, "there is no one who, if he listens to himself, does not discover in himself a pattern all his own." This governing pattern struggles against the status quo and if obeyed urges us to create our own personal masterpiece. "Indeed," Dubos adds, "To compose our character is our duty."

The silent workings of the will has allurements for me, calling forth all the potency of my being in the hope of finding what might be hidden there. Somewhere in that reservoir is the will to be creative—to make something out of that which defies the status quo and instead calls for originality.

I was listening to a psychologist the other night and he kept referring to creative problem solving. He means, I think, that in order to solve some of our problems we must tackle them in untried ways. But what does being creative mean?

Jerome Bruner says it means, "an act that produces effective surprise! The content of the surprise can be as various as the enterprises in which men are engaged. It may express itself in one's dealing with children, in making love, in carrying on a business, in formulating physical theory, in painting a picture." I think the creative enterprise could also include solving a problem, learning to be compassionate, testing frugality or improving and developing respect for life.

A friend of mine was telling about an incident in his boyhood of creativity that helped change his life. He was unconsciously exercising the principle of becoming by being in growing up. He was an ugly kid physically, being cross-eyed and gangling and very self-conscious and hopeless about ever being accepted. Then, when he was about thirteen he went with his dad to visit a friend. The wife of the man of whom his dad was visiting was very pretty, the boy thought, and he wanted very much to gain her favor. Somehow, the boy was led to see that he might do it through being helpful and he offered to carry the groceries, then in helped her put them away in the pantry and other such chores as she would allow. These small acts pleased her. He noted the experience marked a turning point in his life for he found he gained a measure of self-confidence that grew with him through the years. Our young friend started practicing his creative will early.

This simple story illustrates the stuff of which good becoming is made. Simple creativity grows in the mind with wild flower imagination, to be applied as broadly as imagination would allow.

From my own delving into what I do creatively I realize that the ideas of creativity I entertain finally entertain me and that ideas continually beget other ideas.

Creative thoughtfulness can come in tiny packages or in a twinkling of an eye. I chanced to be both the giver and the receiver in a situation regarding a friend of mine this spring. She was to have an unexpected biopsy and I she asked me to represent her at a meeting in Chicago. She was understandably worried about herself and I was likewise concerned. I flew to Chicago on Thursday, attended the meeting and on Saturday called her at the hospital. The nurse handed her the phone to receive my call. "Thank you for calling," she said, "I know your concern made a difference and is it all right, if this week instead of love being the greatest word,—can it be benign?"

When I returned home there was a note in the mail—a second blessing. "Thank you for your caring. My Easter will come early this year for I am a walking arrangement of the Hallelujah Chorus." In one brief sentence my small bit of concern rewarded me a million fold. I learned what a simple thing it is to be concerned in a small way—a smile, a telephone call, a simple act.

This exchange of in-depth giving and receiving, one to the other, is what becoming is all about and I was a step further along the way.

After experiencing this step I was soon to take another. As a child we lived next door to a couple who was childless. Bernie took me in as her own. My mother thought she was really her friend, but I knew she was mostly mine. Forty years have passed since Bernie and I were close. I grew up, had my own family and kept in touch with Bernie through an occasional letter. I learned one day Bernie was dying of cancer. She couldn't walk, her voice was weak over the phone and she received few visitors. Since I had not seen her for years I decided to drive up to see her. The closeness we had enjoyed those many years back returned in a moment and we both knew that the love which was once so rich was still alive and working in both our lives. Our wills were creatively remembering.

There can be specific steps in becoming creative, often leading in unchartered directions. Recently, my neighbor Mildred told me of her experience. About mid-morning her husband came home in a noticeable fit of frustration. "Have you seen the papers I was working with last night? I need them desperately." Mildred jumped up from what she was doing and began helping him search the house for the important papers. They could not find them anywhere. They scoured the utility room and flipped through the newspapers piece by piece; they tore through the wastebaskets and ripped off the bedcovers. They were nowhere to be found. They couldn't have fallen off of the face of the earth Mildred thought, but losing something can be the most troublesome experience, especially when the item lost is immediately needed. "Have you stopped and thought of your day? She asked, "Yes, yes, yes!" "Could the papers be at the office?" "I've already looked there." "Can you do without them?" "Heaven, No!" Her support was anything but support. She thought, "How can I be the most help to my husband at this point? What can I offer him at this hectic irrational time if I can't offer him the papers? Mildred turned the tables around and asked herself, "What would help me if I was this desperate and what would I want my husband to do?" Withdraw! She suddenly realized he didn't need criticism. Obvious, oversimplified helping ideas multiplied his frustration. She could only offer patience in creative withdrawal. "I'm going to stop looking and go back to what I was doing. If something comes to me I'll let you know."

Her husband drove back to his office and as he turned into the parking lot he saw the maintenance boy and he asked him if he had seen any loose papers around? "Yes sir, someone dropped some old papers out of his car into the water. I took them and dumped them in the trash." The papers were retrieved, water soaked and wrinkled—but intact.

This was the time in becoming when the best act was not action but the absence of action. Becoming patient lends itself to becoming less involved more often than more involved. Strangely, the gift of patience is often all there is left for one to do. But it doesn't come easily, especially as one disengages himself from a frantic ensnarement. The husband's frustration concerned the wife, yet she made a noble attempt to withdrawal and from this response of retreat came the slack the situation needed. With awareness of such flexibility our minds and wills can begin to take on new and cross current creativity.

Years ago I read a book whose title intrigued me. It was called The Art of Selfishness—the premise being acts of selfishness are often the best. Soon after the book came out my father had a heart attack. My grandmother was visiting at the time. As they took my father to the hospital my grandmother announced she was leaving and going home—back to Virginia. At first I was aghast; leaving at such a crucial time when surely her son needed her and much was to be done. As I grew older and more insightful, I realized and appreciated her wisdom. As much as she might have preferred to be with her son, she exercised the art of selfishness and decided she would be much more helpful—out of the way. She was a visitor and she knew my mother would be preoccupied with my father so she bade us farewell. A small, unanticipated gesture that at the time seemed cruel and untimely proved to be the type of wisdom and kindness that rose out of selfishness. It required courage I can now appreciate.

My friend Mildred and my unorthodox grandmother experienced the denial of strong aggressive impulses of the will in order to allow for some creative birthing to take place.

There is great discussion these days about 'creative dying' (a strange term), and yet dying is not strange when one considers it as the sequel to birth. If we believe Howard Clinebell, dying is rebirth and is the crux upon which the Christian tradition hangs its faith…the crucifixion always precedes resurrection. We can carry this symbolically to our understanding of the will. Perhaps something in the will has to die to allow for new and fresh experiences to take place. Perhaps it's like Bruner suggests, we have to give up some old habits to actively be involved in a creative pursuit.

While the will can be flexible, pushed and pulled back as needed, it can also be helpful in changing negatives to positives. In the first draft of this book I wrote extensively about the seven deadly sins. I soon discarded them, for I viewed them as negative attributes—large boulders blocking what I was trying to say. But I found they couldn't be that easily disregarded. In real life they come on too strong. Remember them—pride and envy, greed and gluttony, covetousness and sloth, plus that loathsome lust, lurking around every corner. I couldn't ignore these cardinal sins and be true to the task of fully explaining becoming by being. If becoming by being has anything to say, it says it to these elements that so blatantly influence our lives. I was forced to deal with them creatively,

On my desk sits a hermit crab. A real one, mounted by the newest innovation in natural embedment and encased in Lucite. I can't say he is a very pretty creature, but he is a curious critter. There is also a certain universality about him. Found on virtually every coast in the world the hermit crab tells a story common to us all. Having no protective shell of his own he moves into cast off mollusk shells to make his home. His tentacles remain exposed and ready for action, eager to fight off any invader that might want to get at his soft, vulnerable body hidden in the sea shell.

The deadly sins can be our hermit crabs. They hide in an inner shell we have created in order to protect the sensitive parts of our being to make sure no one comes too close, fearful they might see us as we really are.

The long finger-like tentacles, at least the ones I have seen, are generally cast downward. If they were reversed, they would look like a hand ready to be filled. A hand turned upward has the look of peaceful receptivity. If our tentacles of pride, envy, lust and the others could be turned around they might assume a positive stance producing for us, rather than working against us. When we can hold these deadly, devastating elements and view them with the corrective eye of creativity, lust can become love when it is properly motivated, understood, controlled and regulated; pride can become humility, like a workman that needs not be ashamed; and envy can become compassion when the jaundiced eye is turned not to self but to the well-being of others. I think this is what Moreno meant when he said that creativity is a sleeping beauty, but he was quick to add that in order for creativity to become effective it needs a catalyst. He suggested the best catalyst is spontaneity. The very word declares what it is—a sudden spurt of action without directed thought. It's also an onomatopia word; a word that sounds like what it means. And an exciting word, full of zing. The definition comes from the Latin sua sponte which means "coming from within." Most often spontaneity is a blessing, like a burst of applause that comes without notice.

The hermit crab in each of us has the ability to turn itself spontaneously from the defensive negative to the receptive positive.

G. K. Chesterton, a renowned English writer, was once asked what book he would want to have with him if caught on a desert island. Knowing he was a religious man, some suggested the Bible. "No," he said, "I would not want the Bible." "Then perhaps a copy of Shakespeare?" "No," he answered, "not a copy of Shakespeare." "Then what would be your choice?" Chesterton replied, "If I were stranded on a lonely island all by myself I would want a book, entitled, A Manual on How to Build a Ship." When my pride is hurt I don't need a book on humility and how I might attain it, I need first-aid in self-esteem. I quickly call a perplexed friend and offer him support. When I myself need it, I have learned I must find ways of giving it. By giving support I get it for myself and the protective tentacles of my being turn upward and I receive life supporting energy that sees me through the dark spots of an injured pride.

Spontaneity is fun! It can be fun both as a starter and as a response.

Several of the most memorable activities have developed from a quick notion to do something strictly unplanned and often unnecessary. For instance, I will call my husband at the office right before noon and suggest we take a certain friend to lunch that very day. If it works out, it works out beautifully. Had we planned it, we would have worried about where to take him, what would be the best day for all concerned and a myriad of other unimportant details.

A spontaneous gesture such as this has inherent in it intuition. This morning, for instance, I called a close but distant friend. She had been on my mind for three days and it suddenly came to me I could telephone her. I found this friend ready to enter the hospital for surgery and as I hung up the phone I was gratified—for I had followed a spontaneous nudge stemming from intuition—and it turned out to be one of the most creative things I could have done that day.

Creativity need not be a mammoth production. Often a subtle act can be taken and used creatively. I am not the neatest person I know, but occasionally I get the bud to tidy up the place. I don't tackle the entire house. I work methodically on a drawer or a closet, or more likely on the top of my desk. My favorite cleaning job is the silverware drawer. I do like to have the knives, forks and spoons in their own section. The drawer with the spatulas and cheese graters can be thrown in any old way. Any expression of neatness, tiny as it often is, is the means by which the entire house has a chance of becoming presentable.

To paraphrase St. Bernard when he was talking about perfection, "creativity consists in doing common and everyday things in an uncommon manner and not in doing great things." We could add to that and 'doing them in uncommon times.'

Having a special friend who was a prison or war and hearing his stories of food deprivation for months and months causes me to rethink many things. I never go to the pantry without looking over the cans, jars and packaged foods without asking myself, if today, there came a sudden war and no more food would be coming into the house, how long could I stretch the food I now have to feed my family? It would demand of me all my creativity and ingenuity. I would use up the perishables first, then ration the food and discipline our eating according to the best nutrition, while saving back and ultimately hoarding the canned goods and the long-term food stuff. Since I have never had to do this, I've never tested my creativity in this area. I only creatively think about it and if a crisis (heaven forbid) occurs I'd be ready in my mind.

The irony of millions of people starving in today's world of frozen foods, soy beans and concentrates, makes one who looks in his over-supplied larder question fairness. In a mild attempt to strike out at injustice I gave up bread for forty-days. Symbolically, bread is the staff of life and my mental computer went crazy with the wild projections of what could happen if twenty million Americans did the same. Just think of it. We Americans could voluntarily give up luxury foods and simply live off the basics and in doing so feed the world. I even believe we could feed the hungry world on our wastefulness.

Thoreau wasn't forced to go to Walden Pond; his will directed him after he realized that possessions possessed him. He wondered to himself, to the point of experiencing personal creative austerity for two years, if he was the master of his own life? I have a feeling, not as a preachment of doom, but as an honest appraisal of good stewardship, that many people will never see the advantage, much less the necessity of living without. It is not beyond the world of probability that this country might someday live in austerity as it is now living in the utmost of affluence. We might begin in a small way. If we can't give up bread for forty days, can we give it up one day a week?

To read the lives of prisoners of war should be enough to inspire us to learn to live creatively. These men had nothing, yet clothed with the will to survive, they created crude communication systems to help them maintain their sanity through the lonely days and nights. Captain Howard Rutledge in his book of, In the Presence of Mine Enemies, described their method of in detail. "We used tin cups as transducers to tap coded messages through solid walls. For short distances we tapped with fingers; for longer distances we tapped with the ball of fist or elbows against the floor. Other legitimate noises were never wasted—a cough, a sniff, spitting, and/or clearing the throat were converted into simple communication efforts. One specifically ruse was to sweep through a compound, using the broom movements to signal messages to the entire area. Or, if a man walked by another cell, he could drag his little Ho-Chi-Minh sandals in code. When he cleaned out his 'honey bucket,' he swept and cleaned it with a bamboo broom. Often with the guards looking on, men pounded out messages on their pails with the enemy none the wiser." These simple acts sustained these suffering men while at the same time kept them sharp and alert to every sound and opportunity.

Survival calls for creativity. Affluence stifles it.

A master artist was at work in Haarlem, Holland when Mr. Smit, a builder, was called in to make a false wall in a house in order to hide a Jewish family during World War II. Corrie Ten Boom tells how Mr. Smit smuggled in tools in newspapers, bricks in brief cases, paint in milk bottles until the secret place was finished. She describes it. "We stood in the doorway and gaped. The smell of fresh paint was everywhere. But surely nothing in the room was newly painted! All four walls had that streaked and grimy look that old rooms got in coal burning Haarlem. The ancient molding ran unbroken around the ceiling, chipped and peeling here and there, obviously undisturbed for a hundred and fifty years. Old water stains streaked the back wall, a wall that even I who had lived half a century in this room, could scarcely believe was not the original, but set back a precious two and a half feet from the true wall of the building. Built in bookshelves ran along the false wall, old sagging shelves whose blistered wood bore the same water stains as the wall behind them. Down in the far left hand corner, beneath the bottom shelf, a sliding panel, two feet high and two feet wide, opened into the secret room." The author writes that on inspection Mr.Smit struck the wall above the bookshelves and said, "The Gestapo could search for a year and never find this one."

For all I don't know about creativity, I stake claim to one simple truth. Just strike out on an idea with the motivation to succeed and it can be done. I promise further that everything your read about that idea, or touch, or discover or talk about has a bearing on that idea. In fact, the ideas toward fulfillment of that dream come to meet you and each encounter is a rich electrifying experience of becoming. That's how I found the story of The Great Stone Face and remembered the story of Candice Jordan.

The awakening of creativity is the unmistakable inner working of the will in becoming. It fosters the thrill of a new day and the sensation of new currents surging with unsuspected energy through our beings. When this enlightenment comes—we have a new way of thinking and this new mind set leads to adventure and discovery.

Inclined and encouraged as I am toward being creative, I must add one further word—a word we have almost lost in our society—respect. The awesome experience of creating even a modicum of respect has within it the divine, a microcosm of the Great Plan. Creativity can neither be casually formed nor disrespectfully done. It reflects neither caustic spasms nor sarcastic over-tones. It is humbling. And as hard as it is to define, it is even harder to explain and impossible to teach. We can be creative out of our own being and by being become a part of the larger sphere that is designed around the will of the original creator.

In our fictitious story, Ernest lived with a lifetime of respect for his mountain. Had the story been real and Ernest able to speak for himself, no doubt he would have witnessed to the 'becoming' in him…a silent, continual process of the working of the Divine. His commitment had been complete for he set his mind to it. Bruner adds, "The act of a man creating is the act of the whole man."

Thoreau concluded near the end of Walden, "I learned this, at least, by my experiment: that if one advances confidently in the direction of his dreams, and endeavors to live the life which he has imagined, he will meet with a success unexpected in common hours…If you have built castles in the air, your work need not be lost; that is where they should be. Now put the foundation under them."

SUB-STRUCTURES

I remember hearing a spokesman for a personal enrichment program say that to her, there are only three reasons for change within an individual: a crisis, a discomfort, and the beautiful discovery that one can change.

Crisis does alter cases. As I was driving into town recently I heard a newsman interviewing a young veteran back home from the war in Iraq. He had lost both legs in the war and the newsman was asking him what he was doing now. The young man answered, "Well, I have changed my profession. I am no longer practicing law I am going back to college to learn to be a coach. I want to help handicapped children develop their bodies to the fullest." I thought, boy, what a change. A coach—something he would never have decided to do with two legs.

Discomfort also plays a part in change. I thought of a young teacher friend who came into his superintendent's office one day to turn in his resignation. "I can't live as a people pleaser any longer. I've got to be my own man," he said. The discomfort of trying to make too many people happy finally pained him so much he quit the profession and is now set up in business where people pleasing is at a minimum. Like the constant trickle of water, discomforts can become so unbearable they force us to find release.

And then there is the beautiful discovery that people can change. To me, the word can stands out in embossed print. It represents the most hopeful outlook in the English language if not the most helpful. It has power and motion. It far over balances words like 'might' 'ought' 'should.' A positive affirmation can spring into the future, announcing all things are possible.

I first ran across this hopeful word through William Parker's book, Prayer Can Change Your Life. Substitute in his title any other words I mentioned for can and when you do you find not only Dr. Parker's premise weakened, but his idea lacking challenge. His book and his theory sparkle with affirmation simply because of the dynamic word—can. Supported by scientific experimentation, Dr. Parker strongly pinpoints the difference prayer can make in a person's life when the motivating power of can is exercised by the individual. The can factor in exploring prayer power and the can factor in Becoming by Being is the same. One can become.

The question is: are we responsible for change or is change inevitable? Some of us need not worry that we will ever become famous or rich or blue eyed, but all of us accept the fact that we will become old, we will become ill, and we will become, if we live long enough, dependent. From young to old is change---from health to ill-health is change—from independent to dependent is change. The truth is that change is life is certain.

When we cut into a bag of change we find nuggets of change rolling out in various sizes and descriptions. We have viewed change as it comes to us inevitably—the change that comes with the passage of time—the change that is programmed in the divine plan. This change is exciting because it can be anticipated. It can also be predicted and in some measure prepared for. This type of change is commonly accepted.

These are traditionally obvious changes. Not so obvious, until pointed out to us, is the subtle changes that operates in juxtaposition to the obvious. It's the change that is laid on us by outside influences which quietly forces us to adjust and acclimate without our conscious approval or consent. These changes come as changes 'blowing in the wind.'

We can clearly see it in a social way from our history of the past century. If your teenagers were like ours, they confronted you with mail delivery regularly about their opinion of change. "The trouble with you," they said, "is you won't change." But for a parent born in the twentieth century change is our middle name. We have seen more changes in every sphere for living in our time than any preceding generation. The horse and buddy has changed to a super-jet; the pump handle to a faucet; the lantern to laser beam. A person born in the 1800s and dying just after World War II would have seen the coming of the railroad, the steamship, the telephone, the telegram, the electric light, the automobile and the airplane. The rest of us witnessed the coming of television, the computer, the cell phone, email and ebooks as well as the space module. Each one of these marvels has had a direct bearing on our attitude and has changed not only our style of living but our speed of living.

New technology changed us fast. They were such welcomed improvements that the change they brought was gladly received and quickly appropriated. But underlying the apparent benefits of these conveniences that enhanced the quality of life came the less obvious changes that to define or further describe would embrace a subject worthy of book length treatment. Earlier, the automobile alone put power to the wheel speeding our culture headlong into problems of crime, moral imbalance and social deviation. At first these changes didn't seem so traumatic; being helpful they didn't seem immediately controversial, but looking back we can attest to the impact they have made, not only to the outward behavior of society but the subterranean level of individual consciousness. The grain of sand bears as surely on us as the mountain.

More subtle changes come in snow flake varieties. A single encounter with another human being often results in residues of unexplainable change. At a meeting this last summer a woman was talking about her trip to the Far East. During her conversation she mentioned having met several Japanese friends. At this point she stopped and made a very poignant statement, "I am making a list of all the people who have touched my life, because after I have met them I am never the same again." My friend recognized the emotional change that occurred in her with each encounter.

Wallace Hamilton has a sermon which he entitled "You Can't Go Home Again." In it he mentions a quotation from an Ephesian philosopher living back before Plato who said, "You never look twice at a river." This bears thought. And on reflection we know the truth of it. For as Hamilton observed, "No matter how quickly you turn back to look at it, the waters you first looked at have passed, and you are looking at another river." No matter how often I look at my husband or experience an encounter with our son, neither is the same as when I saw him last. The one has been to work, visited with associates, received telephone calls, had lunch with business friends, read a book; the other has been to school, played golf, studied history, spoken to his girl friend. A new person comes back home every night.

A simple insertion of a new word into our vocabulary can bring about a subtle yet long lasting change. A quick review of our day would make this point clearer. The morning newspaper holds for us the particulars of change. Consider what new words we find in the press. Dubai was once a new world as well as a place for me and the knowledge instantly broadened my world and stretched my thinking toward war, isolation, amnesty, freedom and summit meetings, Iraq and détente. From the amusement section I learn about the bestsellers and the latest movies. Each item of current news forms a mosaic of thought and behavior that has a bearing on who I am moment by moment. Snaps and snippets of knowledge and information changes our lives, slowly in an undercurrent of process of which we are neither aware nor are likely to appreciate.

Then there is the deliberate change by manipulation that comes through legislation, social movements and the so-called change agents of our world who pride themselves in offering change to promote the total good. We may not always agree, but the busiest people in the world seem to be the social change movers.

Some of these changes are overtly announced, introduced and implemented in a given time span. We are today in the process of changing our way of thinking about measurements. The American public is slowly being educated to the metric system. In five or ten years the transition may be completer in changing our calculations of miles into kilometers, gallons into liters and replacing Mr. Fahrenheit with Mr. Celsius.

Other changes are as deliberate, but not as pronounced. The ad men and public relations pros are considered the chief change agents of our society. I well remember when President Nixon was making preparations to visit Red China for the first time. Suddenly, all commentaries, news releases and public figures began talking about Nixon going to the People's Republic of China and our entire country changed its attitude about China without consultation or referendum. The word 'republic' sounded so much better to us than 'red' that we barely noticed the sly, yet permanent transition. If anyone was concerned about the transition, few dared to object.

Change comes. Often it comes in unsuspecting ways and most of it is non-threatening. Its principle is written in everything that is living and is readily understood. Knowing this, somehow takes the sting out of whiplash swings of change.

To talk of change, in extremes, is to overreact to the natural evolution of change. Few people turn gray overnight. Circumstances may change in an instant, as in a death of a loved one, but our response to the circumstantial changes, regardless of their intensity, is still slow and progressive. When our children talk of the older generation not willing to change what they really want is approval, acceptance and understanding (although that rarely comes in one package). They are not prepared to understand that change is not a moral issue. Change is living and being every moment.

> *Time goes by turns, and chances change by course.*
> *From foul to fair, from better hap to worse.*
> *--Robert Southwell*

From our bag full of change we now have pointed out a few of the fat and healthy aspects of change—those that call attention to themselves one way or another. There is yet one more—the one my friend referred to earlier as the beautiful discovery that may now be hidden, but merely overlooked. It is the change that we decide to make that has nothing to do with outside overt or subtle influences. It's the change that we consciously and deliberately make in our lives now—for the future. It's the long look of change. It's the change that is called becoming.

There is no debate about can, will, should, ought a person change. Persons will change—in a twinkling of an eye, in the thump of a heart beat or through the passing of one year to another. The joy of discovery to me is to see a person become as he changes—not allowing the inevitable change to be the deciding factor, but exercising the option to become more day by day.

If living is a process that is viewed as constant motion, can motion also be movement. If it can, movement does not spin in its own tracks. It builds and progresses, mainly forward. If we learn from each experience, build with each contact: if we can benefit from awareness and encounter, we can become while we are forever busy about being.

This becoming excites me. Change is already programmed into all creation and that type of change can take care of itself. I can't help the gray hair I now have that time caused, or the wrinkles around my eyes that age and smiles have wedged. Time is definitely slowing my gait and my gallop, but what of the signs of becoming? Can anyone tell I am also working and living at becoming while I am making these life changes? Can anyone tell that I am viewing my mountain every day and yearning to learn the deeper 'soundings' of life? If my face doesn't show it, does my behavior? Am I becoming receptive, gracious, frugal? Am I becoming humble, tolerant, and courageous? Are any of these qualities growing in me as I am growing older, grayer, slower? Change isn't automatically becoming. It is only when the changing process becomes a becoming process. This is the dramatic discovery. We are going to change but we are not necessarily going to become...UNLESS!

We can take on becoming. We've been motivated, we've been shown anew mind set and now all we need is to get to work. We can become more in a minute—the next minute than we are this minute. It's that simple.

But there are some ground rules.

We had been married only two years, our first born was in diapers and I needed an outlet—a diversion to get me out of the house for a few hours a week. I took up art. That is I took up painting with oils. To call it art would be a hyperbole. That was years ago. The diversion served its purpose and though it lasted only a few months I have four oil paintings with my signature in the right hand corner to remind me of that period in my life. This is significant. Those crude paintings are evidence of an experience in which there came a measure of knowledge. I now know an artist outlines first with sepia paint rather than a pencil. I know it is better to stretch canvas than buy a canvas board. If time has changed these methods, I am unaware of it. Pieces of knowledge, simple as these are, are the ground rules of art. To know the ground rules of being and becoming an artist is important. To know the ground rules of creative being while creatively becoming is just as important.

First, let me confess, I didn't find these suggestions tucked away in some nice rule book somewhere. Had I come to this point in the manuscript three years ago I would have had to write, 'Instructions follow.' As I offer these suggestions, I hope you will find others of your own by the simple method I took—of living with the concept. But as I report my findings I do it with the belief that they are sound enough to support all becomers regardless of how high or how broad or how deep the becomer desires to build.

For me, uncommon ground rules made themselves known early in the development—allowableness and receptivity. Both function as abstract forms of preparing for the practice that must follow. I learned this foundation was necessary from my builder friend. He said before a carpenter builds anything he first constructs wooden forms. These forms outline the shape which the cement will take. When the cement hardens, then the wooden forms may be pulled away, leaving the cement that will last. If the forms are constructed properly and the cement poured evenly, the structure has the chance of a good foundation both of balance and solidarity. The outline forms of allowableness and receptivity give the balance and the foundation I feel needed for successful, rewarding becoming.

Allowableness I ran across by accident and receptivity was a gift. The two words may, in fact, be distant cousins but I draw a distinction between them. Both are active words even though to allow has pejorative overtones and undertones. One of my teenagers comes in and asks for the car. Something in me wishes he had never asked, because I hate to turn him down and yet I have no good reasons to withhold my permission. I toss him the keys. This is allowing. But only in part. It's the part that steps aside and watches, in a passive way, events happen. Here allowableness is akin to permissiveness. In this capacity we play the neuter role, amiable and non-interfering. There is a more active side of allowableness and I have come across this as I have been involved in this persistent idea of becoming. It's the allowableness of investment. As we place our money in stocks and bonds, we allow the money to work for us. The concept of investment is to put something in— in the hope of having more come out. Allowableness is the type of active investment in what can happen to us once we consciously make an effort—the idea being—the more we invest, the more results will follow.

I suppose one of the strongest stories about the investment of allowableness was told in Assagioli's book, The Act of Will. In it he speaks of a famous naturalist name Agassiz and his method of training pupils. It seems many of his pupils became renowned for their acute powers of observation and perception and their unusual ability to think about things they see. A tale goes of a new student presenting himself to Professor Agassiz one day. The naturalist greeted him and set a fish, which had been preserved in a jar, in front of him and told him to observe it carefully and then report to him his findings. The student, left alone with the fish, began. He noticed and listed it had fins, scales, a mouth, eyes and a tail. In half an hour he felt certain he had taken the entire fish in and was ready with his report, but the professors was nowhere near. As the time rolled on the young man grew restless and irritable and spent the next couple of hours idling his time. Still no professor.

He went to lunch. He felt disgusted and discouraged and wished he had never come to Agassiz in the first place. Then in order to kill time he began to count the scales on the fish. After that he counted the spines on the fins and then the youth began to draw the fish. In drawing the picture he noticed the fish had no eyelids and he recalled an old adage "the pencil makes the best eyes."

In time the famous teacher returned and was quickly disappointed in the young man's observations. He sent him back to work and this time with the admonition to come up with more. This put the youth on his mettle and he began to work like he had never worked before. He began to catch the secret of observation as little by little new objects of interest came to light about the construction and nature of the fish.

The young man worked with the fish for three days, and years later, after he had attained eminence, he was remembered saying, "that was the best zoological lesson I ever had—a lesson whose influence has extended to the details of every subsequent study, a legacy that the professor left to me, as he left to many others, of inestimable value, which we could not buy, and with which we cannot part."

This young man learned the power of investment when both parties exercised allowableness. The old teacher knew what he was doing. He allowed the boy to stew and become agitated over his dilemma but in the end it paid off, as he knew it would. He allowed for time, for interest, for motivation to work their work. The boy, likewise, though unknowingly, allowed interest and determination to override his temporary frustration and disappointment. He testified that the dividend paid off in spades. The experience was also a major factor in this young man's becoming an acute observer, a process he never forgot.

Closer to home and for me a more concrete example happened in my own home. At one time a status symbol for me was bragging about what I didn't do rather then what I did. I felt I was making favorable impressions by being a non-doer of acceptable universal activities: to wit—television. For years I had watched television with my family. One day I became fed up with the tube. I realized a lot the valuable time was eaten up by watching television and in a gesture of smug denial decided to give up television in large doses. It wasn't long until little on the television programming interested me and soon the TV was only a piece of furniture sitting idly in the house. It was at this point I began to boast, "I never watch TV," hoping people who heard me make this broad exaggerated statement would think I was more seriously utilizing my time. That was the image I wanted them to have. I found in my perverse pride, false as it was, I was denying allowability. I was a barrier to myself. I wasn't allowing TV to be a part of the process of becoming. I was cutting it off absolutely rather than being wise and discerning about what actually is good and worthwhile on TV. Now, at least, I preview the program schedule and find many interesting feature I had no idea were available. Had I not been allowable I would have missed the Adams Chronicles series and the simulcast viewing of the Bolshoi performance of Romeo and Juliet—a performance that enriched my life.

In neither case was I forced. Allowableness is a state of being. It does not force us to do things we do not want to do. But when we are wise and allow these things to work to our advantage, they, in turn, do the work for us and we glean the good from it. Allowability is a freeing attitude that permits all facts to be considered in determining the truth of a situation. It is an absolute necessity for the process of becoming.

Being receptive is different. Unlike allowableness which ventilates opportunity and is a state of being knowingly permissive, receptivity places one squarely in the stadium of active play. And it places one there with a peculiar and special frame of mind. I know of no other mental status in which the immediate benefits are as enormous. It is the deliberate act or intent of the whole being to link itself with the subtle yet powerful forces operating in the vast world of relationship. Like prayer, it is not a spiritual device one calls upon in an emergency. It is not a trait that has neither specific characteristics nor a pre-constructed attitude that formulates the truth before the fact. Receptivity is a state of mind espousing the open-door policy to unknown and unbidden ideas that might emerge from any type of experience.

My friend Charles Ferguson all but claims proprietorship of the concept of receptivity and well he might. He is the only man I know who has written six hundred pages on the subject in journal form as he recorded over a period of two years what happened to him and others as a result of being receptive. He says after his experience of such sustained awareness that he realized he was the wire rather than a current. "As a conductor I let what was out there or up there pass through me and no longer fancied myself as high voltage electricity." He told me this experience of being receptive touched something deep inside him and made him attentive to the contrast between the spiritual and the fleshly. His long experiment with receptivity brought him to say with strong conviction that "receptivity is indeed a quality of mind that permeates the whole being and is therefore at the heart of being in the hopes of ultimate becoming.

Receptivity is not only noticing the contrast of the spiritual and the earthly; it is observing where they intersect. At some point in our mental experience the creature comes face to face with the Creator; at some point in our meditations the things out there reveal themselves in order to make the things down here clear; at some point when we are the wire in which the currents passes we see ourselves as microcosms of all being reflecting imperceptibly upon the macrocosm of eternity. In those moments of receptivity we not only experience awareness—we encounter awareness. Awareness comes to meet us and from this union is born new dimensions in realized becoming. In this regard the experience is spiritual though the setting may be as earthly as a corn field or the corner of Commerce and Main.

That means for me that receptivity is a special condition of the mind that invites ideas to come out of the natural flow. For several months I added my car to the traffic caravan going to and from work on a super expressway. The traffic was always heavy and even at the later hour that I drove I generally could expect to be a part of the great inhalation into the city and later a greater exhalation out of the city. Every driver drove as fast as possible—or as fast as the car in front would allow.

The speed and danger demanded alertness of the keenest turn. The eyes darted and flashed with the speed of the engine. The ears were trained as antennas with radar accuracy. It was at this busiest time that quite unexpectedly an idea began riding with me down the expressway. The idea of mutuality.

The cars and trucks were like a million speeding dancers bowing to each other as they sped down the expressway.

I was driving fast. The truck ahead of me began to slow down. I saw his break lights. I gently applied mine. A poor choice of lanes, I thought, this will slow me down. But I couldn't switch lanes as other cars were zooming past me bumper to bumper. I noticed a white dodge now beside me. I had passed it several times back and it was now in the process of passing me. Without a warning the turn indicator on the truck ahead began flashing to the right and within seconds the huge semi maneuvered itself into the heavy traffic on the other lane. Daylight! The highway opened up to me like a vast horizon. I accelerated and with the offering of a clear passage picked up speed and followed the narrow lane into town.

For the first time I was aware I was part of a great production. All of us on that highway that day were participants in a drama of mutuality. As cars would come onto the stage from the feeder roads others would ease across traffic to the right and peel off as gracefully as they came on. Cars and trucks, wagons and vans, all sizes, all colors, manned by all kinds of people all going in the same direction and synchronized to a similar pattern. In a word it was a miracle. A lovely ballet performed on a highway in beautiful harmony and cooperation, exchanging mutual respect and dignity. Every person and every vehicle had its due space and each timed his performance to match the rhythm of the road.

It was marvelous experience of receptivity and I cherish the thought each time I relive it. I doubt that this idea is finished. When the craze for C.B radios hit in the 80s I saw a similar sociological development in cooperation expressed in the term, "Good buddy." The intent was basically to help and cooperate with the diving public. The good buddy concept placed all drivers on the highways of our country in tune with all other drivers, regardless of personal status. The truck spoke to the Cadillac with ease, not only to wish the driver well, but to be helpful as they offered safe guidance to each other as they drove in and out of cities and townships.

Most C.B fans simply enjoyed it but what they were doing extended further than their two-way sets. The driver with the 'ears' on was past of the whole as he was receptive to the more profound filia of cooperation that transcended all the clever jargon that passes between C. B. receivers.

As I see it, allowableness and receptivity are the forms in which we pour the mixture of our being that helps us become creative becomers. They provide us with symmetry of mind that allow the given structures of our being to roam free—and independently searching for the substance of this world that blends productively with the spirit of our being.

From this theoretical foundation I believe becoming is possible. And though I have used, for my own clarification, the concrete metaphor of a foundation as one builds with wood and mortar, I am mindful that for our purpose foundations cannot be that fixed. Actually, ours is a foundation only of fundamental understanding— a base from which we can build higher and stronger in our imagination.

The beauty of all building is with the design and the practicality, but the enjoyment is in the dimensions. The exhilarating experience of flying is in gracefulness and speed, but it is enjoyable because we are assured we can come back to earth. No one would attempt wings if once airborne he would forever remain so. The qualities of allowableness and receptivity seem to be flexible enough to hold us firm in our building toward becoming while at the same time freeing us of unnecessary scruples and encumbering limitations that keep us earthbound.

As we set our course on such a foundation there appears here and there thermals that keep us afloat. If you've ever been in a glider plane you know the necessity of thermals. They are silent forces that keep the plane aloft and allow it to rise higher and higher in its venture. Thermals, as we have studied, are rising currents of warm air caused by the heat of the surface. These currents form immense air columns ballooning in the sky that lift as a bubble all that comes in contact with them. On these thermals the glider pilot relies. Without them he could not stay aloft but would quickly drift back to earth. With these invisible lifts the glider can soar through the sky for hours.

As we establish ourselves on the foundation of allowability and receptivity we will soon notice currents of energy and swells of unaccountable interest sending our spirits upward. These discoveries are not new, but like thermals, they are invisible—hard to pull from the abstract, but as we feel their presence we begin to rely upon them. These wisps of supportive qualities are elusive as any concept; they are hard to hold like humility: once you think you've got it, you've lost it.

These findings are tricky and work only when someone works them. They have to be applied. Because they are unique they find friends when friends find them. I can only introduce them; it is up to the rest of us to pick up their buoyancy and soar on their backs.

High on the list of 'thermals' is enthusiasm. Everyone seems to know what it is, but it is as nebulous as a handful of air. What is it that sustains enthusiasm and how can we get some of it. Rene Dubos has a marvelous hold on the term, but he explains it theoretically, "…the preclassical and classical Greeks symbolized the hidden aspects of man's nature, in particular the forces that motivate him to perform memorable deeds, by the word entheos— a god within. From entheos is derived 'enthusiasm' one of the most beautiful words in any language. Man today may no longer believe in the divine origin of inspiration, but there are few who do not retain the ancient and almost mystical faith that enthusiasm is the source of creativity."

BECOMING BY BEING

Emerson says that nothing great happens was ever achieved without enthusiasm. He didn't say nothing great happens without enthusiasm, but nothing is achieved. Like champagne, enthusiasm bubbles up within one to add zip to what he does. With enthusiasm a person addresses life with dynamism that both attracts and spreads. It is contagious. With enthusiasm comes energy and with energy comes self-confidence and a will to accomplish. It is never static but alive, moving and insatiable. As a source of personal satisfaction enthusiasm produces its own reward as it mirrors itself in its power to move others. A person is seldom persuasive without enthusiasm, because enthusiasm has one of those fascinating self-perpetuating qualities—it reproduces itself. Enthusiasm sparks enthusiasm.

Fortunately, enthusiasm has two primary elevating features. It is success directed, and is a trait that failure and frustration cannot conquer. The enthusiastic person maintains a power over each earth-dragger. If one possesses enthusiasm the quality becomes as much a part of him as his beating heart. It lives with him and is seen in all that he thinks and does.

Enthusiasm, by definition, is anti-negative. Enthusiasts cannot be negative, fearful, reluctant or easily defeated. They have taken on to themselves the brighter aspects of a positive life. Catching the thermal of enthusiasm is not easy. One doesn't just say, now I am going to be enthusiastic about this subject or this trip or this movement.

My husband once told me that sermons were too far apart. He meant one can easily lose enthusiasm between Sundays. I know what he meant. I can hear a moving sermon and purpose to do something about it, but find by Wednesday I have forgotten both the sermon and the resolve. The inspiration was gone. Enthusiasm cannot stand alone.

When enthusiasm is most effective it is married to an idea. When a person has been captured by an idea, enthusiasm is the result of that union. And if the marriage is a good one the door is wide open for achievement. Mere enthusiasm could well be described as phony, but when it is hooked up with a viable idea and caught up in the upswing of its power it becomes a bulldozer in becoming.

One can be enthusiastic about an idea, a cause, and a purpose. From the memoirs of Nehemiah of the Old Testament comes the affirmation of the power of a great purpose in one man's life. Jerusalem had no walls to protect it from its enemies. Although it was considered a holy city because of the temple of the Lord being built there—few people dared to live among its ruins. Nehemiah wanted to build a wall. He went before the king and asked if he might be allowed to do the work that was in his heart to do.

Artaxerxes issued a royal degree authorizing the rebuilding of the walls of Jerusalem. Letters were sent to all the governors of the province and to the keepers of the royal forests, announcing Nehemiah as contractor and directed all materials to be provided for the gates of the citadel and the wall of the city—and even for the Temple itself.

It seemed a hopeless job. The walls were in ruins, people were scattered, those left were discouraged and despondent. All around the edges were Nehemiah's enemies ridiculing and plotting against him. Four times a demand went up from the enemy for Nehemiah to cease his work…four times the answer came back. "I am doing a great work and I cannot come down." This stirring sentence has echoed down the centuries giving contagious confidence and resolution to people in difficult times.

A person caught in the grip of a high purpose will permit no obstacle to discourage, no criticism to distract and no side issues to pull him away. He will not relinquish his hold on his conviction that what he believes in is worth all it takes to see it through to the end.

Perhaps no other man in all American history mastered this concept as did Abraham Lincoln. He realized he had many enemies. Once when an attack was made upon him for a supposed blunder in the conduct of war, an officer held in his hand official evidence that the slander was completely unfounded, the officer begged the president to permit him to release the facts. Lincoln said, "No, not now. If I were to try to read, much less answer, all the attacks made upon me this office might as well be closed to any other business. I do the very best I can and I mean to keep doing it to the end. And if the end brings me out wrong, ten angels swearing I was right would make no difference." Lincoln's great work was saving the Union. It's little wonder that in every list of great presidents of our country he is found at the very top.

One day I received an up-to-date report on my good friend, Jackie Fisk. She called to announce her good news. She had a new job. The division manager of a company had called her in and began telling her about his million dollar plans for four new retail stores in the city. As they talked, Jackie's enthusiasm spiraled like torrents of water and the manager ended by saying, "I don't care what kind of accountant you are—your enthusiasm has gotten you the job." Jackie is a fifty-seven year old grandmother without a college degree. She is now third in command as comptroller of a bright new company.

I never think of enthusiasm without thinking of Fred Leer, a man who has been struck on all four sides with personal adversities. He lost two wives by tragic deaths and is himself a semi-invalid, having to rest four hours in the middle of each day due to a back ailment. Yet let the executives of the United Way, the Boy Scouts or the pastor of his church need a speaker to challenge their workers in a financial campaign, they only think of Fred Leer.

The idea of becoming by being must ignite with enthusiasm. It must speak to you in terms believable and workable and in neon. The linings of your mind must catch fire with flames lapping around the cockles of your heart and set you burning with the desire to become. If it does, the idea will generate in you enthusiasm needed for the day-to-day business of becoming. A sustained interest depends on maintaining enthusiasm and will, like a nuclear accelerator, recharge the continuing process of becoming.

Imagination follows enthusiasm as a vapor trail. It's the second natural thermal we catch to keep airborne in becoming.

All of us at times have a preoccupation with daydreams and if we could study these dreams we might find sharp clear goals buried in them. Looking even deeper we might understand the activity surrounding the goals to be imagination.

If I am going to be involved in a particularly difficult meeting, fielding questions and offering suggestions toward a solution, I do two things. I do my homework about the subject, and a day or two ahead I generally imagine in my mind the scene. I review questions that might be asked, the possible situations that might arise and the reactions that might surprise. My father taught me this. He used to tell me before he entered a court room he would imagine the trial and possible turn of events. He would role-play them in his mind in advance, inventing counter arguments the opposing lawyers might put forth. From this he would frame his responses by deductive and inductive reasoning, and then logically put forth his plea. He said he did his best to anticipate and pre-construct all the circumstances that might arise in order to best defend his case or his client.

We often fantasize coming events. Admittedly, they do not always turn out as we thought they might in our minds, but I have been equally surprised to discover that, through pre-imagination of situations I have been better prepared to cope with arguments or objections. Had I not anticipated them or dealt with them first in my private thoughts, the argument might have taken me off guard and left me helpless when the time to speak was ripe. Also I noticed, when I take time to pre-think, I am often freer to guide the conversation, direct a line of thinking or initiate a fresh proposal out of the context of the discussion. Either way, I find that pre-thought by imagining what eventualities might arise has always helps me deal with the realities when they do arrive, regardless of how they arrive.

That is why I image myself a writer. For only through the belief, substantiated by daily imagination, could I ever become one. Often I see whole pages already written. I see book jackets and spines and covers and designs. I feel the weight of books and hold imaginary books in my hand as finished products. I hear sentences before they are written and dialogue before it is actually put to type. The mystical power of imaging is what gives birth to inspiration and the will to stay at my desk until the last word is typed. Regardless of how many books of mine are published, I will never consider myself a writer—only a becoming writer.

Near the beginning of George Bernard Shaw's play Saint Joan we find Joan in conversation with Robert de Baudricourt. The dialogue runs like this.

> **Robert:** What do you mean when you said that St. Catherine and St. Margaret talked to you every day?
> **Joan:** They do.
> **Robert:** What are they like?
> **Joan:** I will tell you nothing about that. They have not yet given me leave.
> **Robert:** But you actually see them; and they talk to you just as I am talking to you?

Joan: No, it's quite different. I cannot tell you. You must not talk to me about my voices.

Robert: How do you mean? Voices?

Joan: I hear voices telling me what to do. They come from God.

Robert: They come from your imagination.

Joan: Of course, that is how the message of God comes to us.

The beauty of imagination is its limitlessness. It is as big as the mind. Nothing can hold it or stop it. It has all the room in the world. It can build the tallest bridges, write the great American novel, have a famous reputation for generosity. Becoming by being is living in the image of what one wants to be. It is filling our mind with a prototype, in the belief we will become that likeness. The old apostle Peter told his people to 'be holy.' I asked a friend what he thought Peter meant. He said, "Well, none of us can be holy." I reminded him, "but that is the order—to be holy as God is holy (I Peter 1, 16)." Can we think what would happen to us if we decided to be holy or even imagined ourselves holy? The day would take on a new direction, a whole new atmosphere. Not all of us would come up with the same formula for holiness, but none would deny it would change us considerably. Holiness would make us appreciate the world in a new way in spite of the many differences we might have in the interpretation of the concept.

This is why it helps me to imagine myself as receptive, as patient, as gentle. When I see through the eyes of imagination, I am closer to them than I know.

Related to imagination is meditation.

Meditation is the next thermal lifting us upward toward becoming. Meditation is an exhilarating and deepening experience. It isn't commonly done because it is hard and takes specific time. Yet properly done it corrects the wanderings of the mind, focusing it upon sober and more probing aspects of being. To meditate takes one out of the marshes of distraction and cuts through the thick overgrowth of minutia in hopes of finding a clear path. More than likely a session on meditation will lead to untapped larders of resources—physically, emotionally and mentally. Putting more of the natural capacities of the mind to use it explores the fascinating cul de sacs of the conscious most of us never discover, much less develop or learn to live with.

I understand there are many types of meditative practices, but I must confess a lack of technical and practical knowledge concerning any of them. I can only understand their popularity. From my own attempts to move into the meditative world I can attest to its attraction in self-extension.

One day I was given an assignment roast an honoree. I was told to keep it light, entertaining, yet appropriate to the occasion. Our life-long friend, T. Lee Miller was retiring and his friends were giving him a grandfather clock in honor of the occasion. I took my task seriously and thought of two words—retiring and time. I began to meditate upon those words. A time to retire that has come from a time of continual service struck me and the words that described this came tumbling out—turbulent, tedious, tender, a time of duty and devotion; a time of work and worry; and now the time to relax, reflect, recall—to praise and reappraise the time of his life. The words cascaded from the meditative overflow as I pressed deeper and deeper into the subject. When I was done a measure of satisfaction came over me as if I had researched thoroughly many of the passages one experiences in a lifetime of responsible and respectable service. And I had not left my chair.

One of the purposes of meditation is tapping the crowded subconscious, loosening the grip of the solidified structures that time has fixed there. Allowed to warm in the sun ice melts, so our thoughts and emotions become fluid and flowing, under the spell of meditation, unleashing the essence of creativity.

An article I read years ago was noting the dimensions of the mind, often overlooked in our modern society. According to the author there are actually seven levels of consciousness. A person, interested in raising his consciousness level from the every day zombie level goes through these stages. After working through the lower stages of sex, power, achievement, compassion and conquest of self, that person ultimately ascends to pure ecstasy when reaching the top level, which is the presence of God. I think in the saner moments of contemplative understanding of ourselves we know that the levels are there. We sense them. We even experience them in flashes of insights and in isolated moments, but we are unable to work through them in any coherent fashion and they overlap and blend into each other. The lines are not clear between the layers and we vacillate like the stock market up to one level and then down to three.

But what I gain mostly from any session of meditation is the awesome discovery that there is yet—more. We have not yet begun to guess the infiniteness of the human capacities in areas of personal growth. Our rooms have ceilings, our buildings have walls and our boats have bottoms, but the vastness of the mind transcends all attempts at limitations. It can roam freely to the uttermost. During these periods of meditation (even if I begin in a small way), I glimpse the true essence of becoming that lures me closer to that which must be 'perfection.' Through meditation it surprised me that small satisfactions and tiny accomplishments are viewed as mighty works toward the ultimate of being.

Closely following meditation is the natural expression of prayer. As a thermal it may well be regarded as the strongest silent current bearing us upward. No doubt, prayer is one of the most talked about and published topics in our society. I dare not delve deeply into the theological implications or the denominational differences in the framework and attitude of prayer. None of these concern us here. My interest in suggesting prayer is for the power it affects in our lives, and in the fact that each person feels the need of some divine intervention if he hopes for personal fulfillment.

Again, I draw a distinction between mediation and prayer. Prayer is a partnership arrangement. And it is two-fold. It speaks and is spoken to, if not in words, in intent and purpose. Prayer is directed to a Power or the Source of Power with the hope that the very activity will render a response. Meditation on the other hand, is self-contained. Meditation, on the other hand, is the temporary escape from circumstantial realities for a specific time and for a specific reason. It is dwelling in the world of the mind. Prayer is communion. Granted, meditation often leads to prayer as a natural spiritual extension.

Prayer is not magic. It may be mystical because its power is unfathomable and far-reaching, but it is not a magic trick. Prayer is one of the most dynamic expression voiced by man "Prayer," writes Alexis Carrel, "is not only an act of adoration, it is an invisible emanation of the spirit of adoration, that is to say, the most powerful form of energy that can be brought into play…Prayer is as real a force as gravitation…When we pray we tap the inexhaustible motive force that makes the world go round…"

Prayer performs the function of a transistor between the Creator and the created and is the link that keeps the two in touch and in harmony. Prayer is as vital as breathing for it is the language of the soul. I am convinced that as all creation has within it the innate urge or compulsion to be complete it must align itself completely in accord with the divine design. All of us want the highest that we know. The only way we know to achieve it is to connect, as best we can, to the highest that we know. That connecting power is prayer.

I recommend prayer for another reason—not as a psychological pep talk, as some might suggest, but rather as a back-up to faith. True faith does not come into our thinking without the primal question of 'why.' Prayer is the only means I know of answering that question. The Great Creator did not create randomly or without purpose—thus leaving a 'why' factor for us to deal with. Through the expressions of prayer we have the inside track to all seemingly unanswerable questions. As we seek to connect with the mind of God we have the chance of understanding the mind of God and from his merger comes meaning. Prayer is such a vital part of being and becoming I dare not think of the process without the preparation made by prayer.

These lofty thermals bolster the efforts of becoming by being. Enthusiasm is the match that lights the fire of imagination; imagination is the energy that moves us toward meditation; meditation, then collaborating with prayer provides the power and the beauty of becoming. It can be on a large scale or in the minute by minute, thought by thought, tiny achievement by tiny achievements.

These broad generalized aspirations can be first realized in small direct deeds. I have a discipline problem with myself, but simple awareness will not solve the problem. So, I search for specific things to do. I aim at pin points. When writing, I reduce my enthusiastic vision toward a manuscript from a concept of a book and narrowed it to the job of perfecting a single sentence. I control my day dreaming of publication to the quiet imaging of a word well chosen. I use the art of meditation to stretch the idea into a larger picture making the concept apply to all rather than a few and then I enter the vast world of the infinity that I might, by prayerful contemplation, connect the simple to the complex.

This is a start—a bare beginning, but it builds. From these first efforts—we can open up the hidden caves and crevices of the mind, the space flights of soul and the dream clouds of the spirit. We hold within us an unexplored creation, fascinating to contemplate. To crack it open is the inward journey toward wholeness that will free us to find the outward journey toward becoming. By these subtle changes, these small deeds of becoming we are saved from being changed by the world alone—aimlessly drifting into age and obscurity. Becoming by being rescues every unique self from this amorphous mass and the rebel who denies mediocrity and conformity catches the thermals of life and find he is not one of the many grains of sand who fall through the dry cracks of existence.

SUPPORT SYSTEMS

*L*et me start to fix something around the house and for the life of me I can't find a hammer or the proper sized nail. On a one-to-one count, I am sure we have more hammers and more nails in relationship to Scotch Tape and Elmer's Glue than any thing else—but when I need them—where are they? Their surface insignificance makes them of little value until they are needed and they are the only things that will work. In any building these necessities might be called support systems.

We have finished talking about the natural lifts in life that hoist us out of our lethargic boots—enthusiasm, imagination, meditation and prayer. These are, however, inner directed agents that reinforce the unseen, inside world so the outward manifestations of becoming have the power to work. But they are ambiguous concepts, vague in their job descriptions. They seem to lack handles and direct pointers. They stand ready for use—as does the hammer and nail but they cannot operate alone.

When I had the idea of becoming by being fixed well enough in mind I gathered a group of people interested in setting personal goals. I called this pilot group together and met with them for six weeks. From them came many exciting ideas that have enhanced the original idea and helped further implement the idea forward.

From our experiences together I can now offer specific hooks and racks on which to hang our efforts toward becoming. We discovered each of these specifics to be a tremendous help in the practical application as we became serious about becoming. Granted, if one is going to do this alone, some of these ideas will have to be put aside—one can use only the ideas appropriate for his or her situation. However, if there are even two or three friends interested in working together on this idea, the rewards would be worth the collaboration. But even alone the ideas make sense to the person who is courageous enough to step out and up in becoming. Individuals do it all the time.

From the idea of Weight Watchers I borrowed the practice of weekly meeting. Each week on Saturday morning my husband's Weight Watcher group met for breakfast. He, along with others, would weigh in and his weight was recorded and registered. If he lost weight the group would applaud; if he gained they would not. The thermometer theory prevailed—as the mercury goes up and down—so goes the approval of disapproval of the peers. Never underestimate the influence of peers (teenagers don't have a corner on the market on this). It is one of Americans' strongest incentives and since my husband lost over forty pounds during the process, it was clear that this was a major exercise. Looking back on his experience I think it was one of the key factors, strong and effective enough to keep him on track seven days out of the week for over six months. Had the meetings been monthly I doubt the program would have been as successful as it was. This said to me, the shorter the space between check-ups, the more likely one is to measure up and stick with a program.

Therefore, our group met weekly. On Monday nights at seven o'clock our small group gathered to study and make reports of the progress or lack of it for the week. After each member set his or her goal, I designed a chart by which we made personal evaluations and peer evaluations—the idea being—as I score myself I can measure it against how others score me. This method was later abandoned because it came to be unrealistic. Many members could only guess at another person's progress. Many times a person felt he or she had made progress when it wasn't apparent in the eyes of another. Becoming by Being was first realized at this point as being a private process. Marked achievement could not be measured; it could only be experienced and that, most of the time, was known and felt by the individual in the depths of his or her own evaluation.

Nevertheless, the group's coming together provided a necessary function. The meetings served as a recharger. Each person needed another person to emotionally applaud him, encourage him, but most of all—to expect him to fulfill the contract he had made with himself and the group.

In the first meeting each member stated his or her goal and the race was on.

The sense of expectation came on strong. We discovered that most of us measured up to expectations if the expectations came from persons or a person one respected. Some sociologist call these people 'significant others,' (we use that term differently today.) None of us desires to disappoint, none of us disappoints deliberately. On the contrary, all of us operated with the primary drive to please and to gain favor and to fulfill our goals.

For myself, let the right person expect me to do something, and the chances are I'll over-react and be far more on the outside (for show) than I am on the inside. But the point remains—by the very act (purposefully done) of being, I was on the road to becoming. If this makes sense, this is the core and kernel of the becoming by being concept. Teachers know this. It's an essential operation in teaching children—"Johnny, you are really a hard worker, Pete, you're the best help I've ever had, Janis, honey, your little mind is working all the time." Most of us, as children, would have turned inside out for a teacher who thought we were 'something.' Why do we drop this natural means of motivation when we are adults, husbands and wives, bosses and employees? Are we too sophisticated to admit that we like to be liked and secretly pine for the fine qualities that make us likable?

Early in this program the group said they wanted some kind of prompter that would remind them of what they were about. They wanted something they could see or hold in their hands. This 'thing' was a reminding devise similar to a rock in the pocket or a string around the finger. They wanted spot announcements that would remind them to think 'becoming,' before they acted. They spent a week searching. The next week one member brought back the idea of writing out her goal on small cards and placing them in her billfold, on the refrigerator door, on the mirror, under the desk glass or wherever it might be seen regularly and instantly. This sore thumb concept turned up in the strangest places. One member tied his slogan around the bathtub faucet so he could soak and think; another wrapped her card around a lipstick tube; another sealed one on her car dashboard; and another used it as part of her breakfast table decoration. The best place I thought at the time was to place a reminder card on the clock.

It seemed the more reminders the better the performance.

PATIENCE. I wrote in bold letters. I taped this single work in various places around the house for my benefit not thinking other eyes would be interested and curious enough to question me and then hold me to my commitment. Our daughter was the first to notice my reminder and asked about it. I patiently explained the idea to her and knew when I did I had committed myself to following up—when she was around, at least. It's like deciding to have a dinner party, you put if off as long as possible, then make the first call inviting the first guest—then you're committed. I realized in my becoming I now had other eyes as judge, jury and sentencer the moment I posted the notice and told my curious daughter about my experiment.

The next day I felt that decision's full impact. My daughter and I were out together in the car running somewhat late for an appointment. Traffic was particularly heavy. The shortest distance and the fastest route were by the super highway. I sped onto the highway with a racing motor and traveled about a mile before the traffic slowed me down to the point I thought I could walk faster. I inched along and at the first exit I spurted off the highway onto the service road feeling I could make better time traveling it. As I did I glanced over at my daughter sitting beside me and caught her head penduluming back and forth. "Patience, mother, patience!" I was duly censored and I knew it.

To hold a goal in front of you is work and to maintain enthusiasm with momentum is a constant uphill battle. When we would meet on Monday nights our group was quickly fired up. Excitement ran high for a day or two. But by Thursday, at the most Friday, the inspiration began to lag and the daily influx of distractions took their toll in our efforts toward becoming.

This need then resulted in our next assignment.

We were to call one person in the group every day. Alcoholics Anonymous uses this method extensively and it works. When a person is feeling vulnerable, unsure, discouraged, or on the verge of falling off the wagon the alcoholic always has a friend to call. This friend responds quickly, either coming to his house or continuing to talk to him on the telephone until the dangerous depression passes. In our case, we didn't necessarily need someone to keep us from doing something bad. "How is it going today?" The question, the answer and the voice of expectation produces a temporary inoculation against the dull, unexcited moments and gave new spirit that often lasts until the next call. Much came from the personal visits over the phone that would never have developed simply from group interaction. The required calls made life-time friends. When a person's need and joy becomes a part of another's growth that person becomes very special.

Then there was the disturbing assignment that few enjoyed and at first objected to, but resulted in all kinds of exciting feedback. Go and tell! The members were asked to tell someone about what they were doing about Becoming at least once a day. Exposure! Burrr!

The assignment was simple but difficult. This meant they had to explain the program to others, and though difficult at first they soon learned how to turn a conversation to the subject with ease. The object wasn't to spread the word about becoming by being; the objective for the assignment was fathoms deeper. Until every one could explain it, they didn't fully understand it. To explain the idea made the idea come alive. The members soon discovered that explanations took the idea out of the realm of the abstract and often became the center of many of their conversations. When something works it is news, and this worked

This idea came from my husband. During the time he was on Weight Watchers I noticed in every gathering of friends it wasn't three minutes before someone would comment, "Are you losing weight deliberately or have you been ill?" That was all the crack my husband needed to get his pitch in. He quickly began telling about WW in glowing, supportive terms. Recruiting converts was not his intention; his big gain in telling about the experience was the reinforcement he received toward dieting. Having people notice gave him the added stick-to-itiveness to drop his weight, ounce by ounce. It was a moral victory as well as a physical one and I felt, since people are not as observant of the acts of becoming, in subtle settings, the idea of telling someone else had to be deliberate. It kept the idea in the air and actively present in the members' minds. When others knew about it and commented this was a spiritual victory for becomers.

Telling someone else served still another purpose. It offered instant green lights.

A writer friend was telling me of the many personal messages he received at Christmas time, most from long time friends who had known him through the years as a writer and editor. Invariably they mentioned their own longings to become a writer. He, thoughtfully, wrote back and offered them the idea of becoming by being with the advice to simply go ahead and be a writer today, tomorrow and the following day. He added, "One day you might be a writer. Don't settle for longings, start today."

This can be good advice for any age with any assignment and it can begin at any juncture in life. As I write this myself I repeatedly realize the entire reason for writing this book is to tell those who aspire to do or be—to begin this minute being it. As I mentioned before, what other way is there?

There is yet another motive for the telling. Telling clears out the cobwebs of uncertainties. As long as we keep our becoming a secret, we are not committed and can back out, and the fullness of its impact is lost. We must be sure we have grasped the idea. As ideas are further exposed and brought to light other ideas emerge. From our group and from every direction, exploring ideas became an enlarging experience. Once we told we no longer lived as if we didn't know.

High on our list of helpful devices was the Bible. The Bible became the fuse box of information and inspiration. The old book, shelved for so many years, was picked up and dusted off. Only this time with research in mind. The members of the group were going a-huntin.' I loaned more concordances, Bible dictionaries, topical interpretations and other references of the Bible than ever before. Everyone began reading the scriptures with the intensity of a mystery novel. Each one was anxious to get the details, the direct word, the hidden secrets and the full undisclosed story sequestered in the Bible. "When did they put that in the Bible?" was a common comment. Or, "I've read this stuff forever but I it didn't say this to me." Or, "When you've got something specific to look for you can find it—the Bible talks about anything you want to talk about."

All translations and paraphrases of the Bible were used and recorded. Members on their own began keeping notebooks. Some began typing up scriptural references they could use as reminders. Often one member would find helpful suggestions for another member from the scriptures and would pass them along. The Bible became a pantry of resources that seemed never empty. Each week, new revelations were expressed that had come directly from the scriptures. From my own list on patience I cherished these:

And as for what fall in the good soil, they are those who hearing the word, hold it fast in an honest and good heart, and bring forth fruit with patience.(Luke:8, 15).

More than that, we rejoice in our sufferings, knowing suffering produces patience, and patience produces character and character produces hope (Rom: 5. 3).

For you have need of patience, so that you may do the will of God and receive what is promised (Heb: 10, 36).

The Bible became a human book filled with people similar to ourselves, struggling to make the most of life, in difficult and frustrating times. Our group identified with our new scriptural friends and as we did we began to see our actions and attitudes dealt with from a spiritual viewpoint. True, the Bible often pinned us down, but in every case, it also picked us up. The Bible repeatedly said: go and do, run and tell, come and follow, indicating no longer do we have to be satisfied with the status quo—"be ye therefore, even perfect!"

A common human failing was surprisingly brought out in our search through the scriptures. We don't see things unless we look for them. How often we overlook road signs on familiar highways. Not until we are going someplace in particular do we begin watching for signs to get there. Regardless of how poorly and obscurely marked, if our destination depends on signs, we find them. When we do, these significant signs stand out as Moses' burning bush. The Bible cleared up the road markers.

Thus we found the scriptures to be endlessly helpful. There is no limit to its vast wealth of inspiration, identification and insight within it. The more we read and studied, the more we found.

A serious student, dedicated to finding answers, can spend a lifetime in search of these answers in the Bible. For most of us, the Bible came down from the old shelf permanently and moved in with us, not as a visitor or stranger, but as a companion on a continual basis.

Lastly, we began using other literature and various types of outside reading. We became sponges soaking up the knowledge of the universe, if the knowledge could help us be what we had set out to be. Early on, I had promised the group, that once they had set their goal and had become infected with the idea almost everything they picked up, in the way of reading material, would pertain to it. Not only did this prove so, but the members of the group began exchanging books and ideas like recipes. One would bring a book that had spoken something to him and when another member would break in and say, "That sounds like a book I'd like to read." Business picked up at book stores and libraries and the few who admitted, at first, they rarely read a book, much less one all the way through, were getting with the reading program. One mentioned after a few meetings, "Has all this stuff been here all along and I just didn't now about it?" We were thrilled with the discoveries. To some it was like going back to school—they rediscovered the library, the research catalogs, the reference shelves, the card catalogues and the reader's guides and the internet. Before we knew we were not only reading we were studying a new range of unexplored treasures: the Bible, commentaries, newspapers, funnies, the classics, short stories, books on quotations and theological and philosophical writings and articles on the internet. We were alive with learning.

I couldn't help but recall at the beginning of the session some of the members asking, "How much work is this going to require?" I now think of this natural hesitancy. If they now considered it work they never complained. It wasn't work. This was something working.

With all our support systems working separately or in concert we realized they could only provide us with the push and shove to action. We had to believe the idea workable and act accordingly. This, we learned, was a faith assumption—an intellectual persuasion that operated in the realm of visualized possibility. As the will provided the chief motivation the power to believe served as back-up machinery. All other systems worked to keep us on track.

We learned it took imagination, exaggeration at times and encouragement and an occasional disappointment. But we all proceeded by faith—until that faith became more a fact with each new day.

AS FOR ME

My father had an accident on the golf course years ago. Due to some maintenance work on the course a heavy chain had been drawn across two points blocking off a dangerous area. My father, unfamiliar with the project and lacking knowledge of the situation, drove his golf cart through the chain nearly cutting off his thumb. As he was in the hospital having the thumb sewn on the thought came to him that the next few days were going to be hell to pay and he would be in pain and highly nervous. He thought of his recurring desire to quit smoking and reasoned that as long as I am going to be in pain, nervous and uncomfortable from the sore thumb I might as well use this time to quit smoking and endure the pain, discomfort and nervousness only once. He did and it proved successful for him. He did not smoke the rest of his life.

A similar rationale came to my mind when I began experimenting with the thought of becoming. As long as I am going to be involved, I reasoned, I might as well take on as much as my discipline quotient would allow. Instead of starting modestly and building up, I outlined a full-scale program for myself. If it took discipline I wanted discipline to work in as many areas as it could stretch.

The three areas I chose I felt would correct as many of my general needs as possible. It didn't surprise me to discover, once I selected these areas, they had a natural kinship and commonality. As I looked at myself, I found a quick temper, high restlessness and a predilection to say what first popped into my mind, all added up to my need for patience, diligence and a controlled process of thinking. My weaknesses were as interrelated as, I later learned, my wholeness could be.

I quickly noted that all the things I wanted to be did not stem from innate or natural leanings. They were, in fact, appealing because they were opposite qualities from those I knew I possessed. I wanted patience because I had always enjoyed a life full of high-spirited impetuosity. I wanted diligence because I was quick, often haphazard about my work, time and speed oriented, eager to do the job and get on to another one. I wanted to be a thinker, not because I didn't have thoughts occupy my mind, I did, but only in idle moments and in contemplative moods. I wanted to be a thinker, not to slow down my actions but in order that my actions might have in them rational cognitive support. When I thought of this tendency toward my desire for the opposites of what seemed natural to me I realized I was seeking wholeness.

Wholeness was the coming together of all part often from diverse points, filling into the missing links of my total being. Naturally, I wanted what I did not have, not that I was unhappy about what I did have. Frankly, I was pleased with some of my abilities, especially the one to work fast and to think quickly on my feet. I was pleased to have the energy coming from a high spirit, but in order to keep the good qualities from showing their seamier side, as often they did; I needed their complementary counterparts to balance the whole. Never satisfied with the given tendencies, I was eager to incorporate every additional quality that might enhance and complement and refine the qualities that I now have. I wanted patience, not because I wanted it, but because I needed it to balance my impetuousness. I wanted diligence because I needed it to counter and calm my restless tendency. I wanted to be a serious thinker, not for show, but because I needed the grounding of what mental depths could do to extend the thoughts beyond the immediate.

I wasn't aware at the time but as I began to practice them, these three attributes became, of themselves, another peg in the overall principle of becoming by being. Not only did I need them for better behavior, as it developed, they could be generalized to apply to my total self. When any one of them was working, all worked. When one was lacking, all seemed to be. As I began to apply patience, diligence easily followed, allowing time and the proper atmosphere for thought about the subject. If I started with the thought process, patience was readily at hand, along with diligence, when it was required. Strange, but it seemed I could begin with any of the three attributes, and while in the process of working with one the others joined in naturally. I felt I had created a team; any one of which would begin the process of helping me work out my becoming unified.

Now I never had any formal instruction on how to be patient. What I had learned from life was how to be impatient, and this was gleaned from the negative responses to what I had done or said. Hard words, unjust criticism, sarcasm and rejection kept me cautious but they were not the stuff of which patience is made. My world was a world of action and reaction. Patience seemed passively sissy, inane and powerless.

As I matured the need for patience took on credibility, but the foundations patience were not set for the having. I had to learn about patience by unlearning impatience, starting back with the first grade. And I was quick to note, adopting a course in patience closely resembled taking an overdose of caster oil. It demanded immediate attention.

The need for patience was around every door, hovering around every situation; and let it be said right here, that once any of us decide to adopt a thought or follow an idea, that idea inundates us with its presence. Almost before I could fully decide, patience was having its way with me. It called to me and beckoned me to let it in my life.

To be patient meant I had to forego anger, to forego having my way and to give the matter my fullest time and attention. None of these, save anger, did I anticipate. I was willing to be patient, I thought, if it didn't interfere with my pre-established pace and the way I did things. But that is exactly what it did. It interfered on every hand and had, for all appearances, the intent to change my personality. To be patient meant I had to conquer anger, selfishness, and control of time. Good grief!

I had to begin by unlearning. As a child I was taught to verbally fight. Fighting was a sport in our family from parental arguments and sandlot scraps to the court rooms. My father was a lawyer, and by definition, a person cocked and primed for battle in verbal wars. He was also a marine and that should shed light in abundance on my formative years. Fighting involved taking sides and defending one's position. By precept and strong example the challenge of being pitted against an idea, a person, or a situation was staged and set in my early training. As a result I was a good debater in school and as my relationships grew I became more astute at making points emphatically. Anger was a natural kid sister and often a defense when my opinions were neither appreciated nor accepted, much less challenged. Anger, I learned, was the bell ringer for patience.

One of my earliest escapades in dealing with anger is still window-pane clear. I was reared in the age of switches—those small branches snapped from lower limbs of trees and bushes that parents used to apply punishment. On one occasion my mother, eager to punish me for some misdeed, ordered me outside to get a switch, which she planned to use immediately. She was fiery mad. I was fiery mad, too. I went out and with much ado cut the largest limb I could manage from the chinaberry tree. I dragged it into the house, leaves and all, past the porch, through the back screen door into the kitchen and on to the bedroom strewing roughage all the way. This infuriated my mother. She sent me back out to get another one. This time I nipped off the tiniest twig I could find, flimsy enough for a feather to bend, and brought it to her. She was livid. Screaming, she sent me out, once more, with no uncertain instructions, for an appropriate switch.

This is all the story I recall (psychiatrists say we forget unpleasant things that happened to us in early childhood, though no doubt, I got my legs duly burned). I relate the incident to show my tendency toward rebellion fostered by anger. Although I don't remember the outcome, I can distinctly remember the feeling of anger within me. I was so angry with my mother I was saying to myself all the while bringing in the massive branch, "Go ahead, kill me."

A strong memory to live with.

From those dim but poignant days grew my familiarity with anger, and as I began my journey toward patience, anger had to be formally and finally dealt with. For out of anger sprang impatience. Did I correct the anger and by that correct my impatience? Or did I correct my impatience and through a natural consequence, correct the anger? I did not know, but I felt I could deal with anger if I thought that it was the by-product of impatience rather than impatience being the by-product of anger. Dealing with patience was the only positive approach I had.

It helped to learn that patience was not only a virtue high and lifted up; it was also an art. As an art, I could use it as I might a paint brush, as the instrument used to create patience. The art of patience is a working arrangement. The virtue is something else, indeed. I couldn't seek a virtue—I had rather the job of trying to perfect an art. I could learn patience only by applying the techniques I thought added up to becoming patient; awareness, hesitancy, deliberation. I had to practice practicing. No way could I hope to achieve patience without practicing patience and using all aspects I felt made up the whole of patience. Yet the question curiously followed. What does one do to practice patience—count to ten; bite one's nails; walk around the block? A cartoon of Charlie Brown comes to mind. Lucy was walking through the house in the first frame, "I give up." The second frame: "I can't stand this family, I give up." The third frame, Charlie Brown is sitting in front of the television and he says, "Where does one go to give up?" Where does one go to find the techniques to be patient? Are there directives, specific dos and don'ts? As I began being patient, in little ways, insights appeared to help me—and soon I was discovering the ingredients of patience through the enactment of the art itself.

Warnings appeared. In my case, the warnings to anger became a guide to patience. This, I learned specifically from my son. As a young golfer he was a throw-the-club type. His anger often got the best of him, and once it did, it destroyed his concentration and subsequently the remainder of his shots. His father and I counseled him to watch his temper and suggested if he was ever to become a professional golfer, self control was absolutely essential.

One day he went out and on his return we questioned him about his game and his disposition. "Did you get angry?" I asked. "No," he said, "but I felt it coming up on me." A key! There is a warning signal to anger. It's that hot surge of lava bubbling inside that one feels when he is threatened. This warning sign was what I was looking for. If we have a warning—we have a choice. And this warning we could feel instantly and name on the spot. Threat!

The second warning followed quickly. To deliberately decide to choose anger made adequate room for patience. We have to give patience time and space—room to be. One can't be stingy with time and ever be patient.

A phone call. It was amiable at first, many happy exchanges, then the reason for calling, followed by an active discussion of the issue. In the midst of my friend's speaking I interjected a word, "Don't interrupt my train of thought," the man lashed back. Wow! My instinct was to—but I gave the situation space, a second, then another second, time for me to think instead of react. He went on. The warning had come. I felt the threat, but I gave the situation the moment it deserved. Unless he reads this and remembers he will never know that an angry incident was aborted. This was not an earth shaking accomplishment, but in that moment I achieved a significant step forward by giving an extra span of time and room, and allowing an unfortunate incident to slip by without losing our status as friends.

Other factors soon became apparent. Objectivity was required and became a force in planning my strategy toward becoming patient. I had to learn to think outside myself. All issues had to be viewed impersonally. And that is no small trick, especially for one as self-oriented as myself. The hardest was the closest to home—with my family and close friends. It's a shame intimates have to be victims of one's experiments in becoming, but as yet I've found no adequate or better substitute. To be objective with compassion was my alternative to anger with emotion and my family was prime target.

My parents soon became unaware subjects of my becoming objective, while stretching for patience. When I visited them last, I asked myself. If I were their friend rather than their daughter how would I treat them? Strangely, my answer was in favor of the friend. I would have been infinitely more patient as a friend, but as a daughter I was hard put to tolerate their occasional critical attitudes. So, to them, I became a friend in order to be objective. When they began fussing about the length of the boys' hair or the lack of length of our daughter's skirts I approached it as an understanding friend. I didn't try to explain to them that times had changed and that it's tougher to raise children today than it was in their day. I allowed them to vent their disappointment and disapproval of me as a mother and of our children as human beings and offered them a smidgeon of patience by helping them generalize their feelings to all the grandparents of the world. From this, I learned to my eternal joy the value of people who love me most. I didn't love them out of duty, as a daughter, I loved them for themselves as one might a devoted friend.

At home one morning I decided to take note of particulars causing impatience in my life. The list ran something like this: lateness, lack of manners, wastefulness, and gluttony. As I looked back over the list I made an instant discovery. Situations didn't bug me—people did. I am impatient with people's foibles and eccentricities when they don't measure up to my standards, and this is the critical point. As I thought about this, I came to realize that situational incompatibilities must be handled with maturity. I wasn't impatient with car trouble, late planes, poor postal service. These things were not my responsibility. People irritated me and caused me to be impatient because I felt, for the most part, they were a responsibility of mine.

Soon after I began to look for these same signals to impatience and examine them closer for clues to why I felt so responsible.

I am never on time. I am always early. I cannot bear people waiting on me. It is difficult for me to understand why everyone isn't as punctual as I am. But they aren't. My husband, for instance, is happy enough to be the last one at a party. He feels he's done his part if he arrives just in time to catch the plane. His feathers aren't ruffled if he has to wait on people.

Manners strike me in the same way. Our youngest son's manners lacked much to be desired—at home, that is. Others told us he was a perfect gentleman away from home. But he felt at his house he could eat without a shirt, leave his bed unmade, or flip the TV channel when someone else was watching. If not here—then where?

As I reviewed the irritating human qualities that burned me up, I began thinking of ways I could be relieved of this assumed responsibility. I began with the obvious. In referring to any offence I moderated my voice; I said less than usual and with fewer stings; often I acted as if they didn't bother me. But this was done without graciousness which was only holding my anger in check and not relieving the pressure of impatience. I was as impatient as ever, only expressing it differently. Band-aid treatment at best, I wasn't getting to the source of the problem.

Then it came to me I was being a block rather than a sponge. When these moments hit me I couldn't take it. I blocked and sent them back hurling faster than they had been given. I was neither making allowances nor exercising allowableness. Nor was I allowing the other person's right to his own ways. I was judging by my own eyes, and it was categorically unfair. I began trying to become a sponge absorbing, little by little, the irritations about punctuality, manners, wastefulness and all the rest. From the role of teacher, mother and judge I began to seek ways to move into the role of colleague, companion and fellow learner. It's hard to break the blocks of pre-set concepts and habits, but patience demanded it and I reluctantly, but only gradually, began to make the turn around.

The last thing I want to say about my efforts toward patience is that it became easier when it began to have meaning.

When patience took on meaning it pushed my becoming to a new level of behavior rather than to a new type of behavior.

For most of my life I thought I operated fairly successfully without patience. To want it badly enough to work for it required, not only a need, but a reason. I needed a philosophical reason. Emotionally, I knew it would help relationships, and physically I knew it would keep my blood pressure down and perhaps, these should be reasons enough, but I needed to be convinced that patience had innate value, worthy of my time and effort to acquire.

But insight into patience did not appear all at once, I doubt it ever does, nor can it ever be complete. Actually, I proceeded on blind faith, trusting it was the best thing to do. I chose to be patient to control my anger because I was too old to ignore anger any longer. I also hoped I was too intelligent to let it grip me forever. My need for meaning came as I acted upon patience. As I lived with it on a daily basis, it took on the characteristics of a gift, and as a gift it brought meaning.

Patience produces. Never have I been a part of a situation in which the use of patience was not profitable and pleasant. Of all virtues, it seems to me patience ranks the closest to purity. Love can be lust; kindness can be do-goodism; gentleness can be self-indulgence, but patience stands on its own merit. Time does not rob it of productivity and circumstances do not diminish its value—in all cases, patience demonstrates meaning born from its own performance. I came to respect patience as no other and now that I recognize it in various forms in other people, I admire its versatility and its healing presence.

Secondly, I pursued diligence. Until I did no one could have told me diligence could ever be delightful. When I thought of diligence I thought of details and details meant work. But I discovered diligence has distinctive characteristics all its own and should be brought out of the moth balls and back into fashion. It is one of those 'must' qualities that acts as a prerequisite to all achievement.

Diligence, by definition, means attentive perseverance; a steady and earnest application to a subject or a pursuit. It isn't of itself, work. It is the attention one pays to what one wants to do with a steady eye toward the future. The results may be work, but diligence is only the seat belt fastened around the seat holding a writer to the page, the artist to the easel or the musician to the instrument until the task is completed.

Years ago a friend reminded me that one should not fret about the number of chores one has to do in a given day. Only do them one at a time, she suggested, and before evening falls most of the work will have been done. I've used this theory on many busy days and find by applying the steady turns of diligence, the jobs generally grind themselves done.

Ernest, in our story The Great Stone Face, made a morning and evening vigil to his beloved mountain. I would suggest it was diligence that led him there and kept him coming back. The process of quiet diligence is caught in its full cycle in this story for the perseverance to any sustaining venture holds one captive until the aspiration and attainment are one.

Personally, I didn't have a natural disposition toward diligence so my first duty was to find a working relationship with it. I used every trick in the trade. I rewarded myself with certain hours of steady work, set standards and goals of production, worked out time tables and made appointments with my project. I even engaged a carrel at the library in which to do my work, freeing me of household distractions. These were tricks of manipulation. I used the mental tricks as well. One day a friend said to me, "there are those of us waiting for your book." Another said, "When are they calling for the manuscript?" Still another, "Will your book be out by Christmas?" Yes, yes, yes! Someone needed me to hurry. There were those out there who were waiting for me and I must not disappoint them. I must be diligent.

Then I used the clincher. I openly committed myself in public. The day I brought the book idea out of the study and into the community I knew I had to keep at it until it was complete. I wasn't going to embarrass myself by being simply a talker. I had to prove that I was really doing something and had a good reason for declining luncheon dates, bridge parties and shopping sprees. After making my excuses I added—"and it's a darn good, too," which put me on my mettle. I couldn't get by any longer with sloppy work, half baked ideas and shoddy follow through. I had to be what I said I was going to be and do what I said I was going to do and guess what? I became diligent by default. I noticed I would become so engrossed in the work of the moment that diligence disappeared into the flow and enjoyment of working. Diligence put backbone to my efforts and soon that backbone was standing on its own. Samuel Johnson said, "What we hope ever to do with ease we must learn first to do with diligence."

As I practiced diligence I slipped into the problem of preciseness. Detail work bores me. It frustrates me and exasperates me. High restlessness does not lend itself to the love of details. Yet to be attentive to a pursuit demands a measure of preciseness. For instance in writing, way before I had a computer, I had to learn to number the pages, spell my words correctly, watch my punctuation. This was detail work down to the last jot and tittle. It drove me crazy. I was happy enough to pour out the ideas, elaborate extensively if necessary, and offer example after example, but I cared less about the minutia that went with it. I had to make myself. As hard as it was to stop a thought at the end of a page, I would, and while the paper was still in the typewriter ease it back up and make as many corrections as I could while it was fresh on my mind. This didn't solve all my editorial problems by any means, but it squelched my devil-may-care attitude toward details and gave me an appreciation of a finer literary style. "Care Cures Carelessness" a wise admonition from one of my favorite books on writing, is now on a post-it note over my computer. As my notes remind me to be patient, so this special word has caused me to pause, look up a word or rephrase for clarity. My next project may be to add consistency, because I find I clean up many details, but not all of them. There is still work to do.

I discovered diligence goes beyond the drudgery of massive details. Diligence possesses a future. When I am part of any long-range planning I see diligence working at its best. Sometimes the ways and means of long-range planning are not known in advance—a time line is all one has. And often diligence is the connecting factor that crunches the dates and the data together in order to meet the deadline.

There is always a reason for diligence. When people are diligent they are diligent toward something. As a child our oldest son was project oriented. He was either developing pictures, rigging his room with electronic equipment or experimenting with chemical formulas. His grandfather dubbed him a 'finisher.' He said, "That boy always finishes what he sets out to do." At the age of twelve he decided to build a telescope. This was no mean project. To grind a lens requires hours and hours of tedious motion, rubbing glass against glass. The grinding had to be so exact that one extra swirl of motion could distort the lens and thus make it useless. At first the project was exciting to our son, he was happy to be in his room grinding away, but as the days passed, the monotony of it dampened his enthusiasm and he fell back on diligence to keep him going. Funny though, as soon as the end was in sight his enthusiasm returned and he was eager to get home from school to work on this special piece of glass. His diligence rewarded him, for after all these years, he still has the telescope he made as a youngster as a reminder of the time he spent out in the back yard searching the heavens and viewing the stars through this finely ground magnifying lens.

The track of becoming by being is thus oiled and greased by the lubricant diligence. As diligence is applied on a regular basis, the efforts toward the goal has a smoother passage. It stands to reason that diligence is a major contributor to all achievement.

To discuss thinking as a trait to be sought may, at first, appears out of the scope of becoming. The tendency of our culture to place thinking ability in the category of the givens, as one is given blue eyes or brown eyes, is to underestimate the range of creativity. We know we can be educated and acquire knowledge and information, but we feel being a 'thinker' falls into the business of native talent with special qualities given. It is not something to aspire. It also may have the taint of arrogance and haughty irrelevance, but I maintain there are valid grounds for my pursuit. You see, I fall into the category of people Kenneth Barnes talks about when he notices that most of us are primary doers who stop to think; we are not primary thinkers who act our thoughts. If I could reverse this trend in myself and maybe others, I might begin to unite the two—so long divided—thinking and doing. We then could establish integrity between the two.

Many of our minds are in a state of uncertainty. A good line my friend gets off is, "I am of two minds, neither of which is settled." The rest of us feel if we only had two minds we were lucky. There is a sequence from Fae Malania's delightful book, The Quality of a Hazel Nut, that describes our apparent double-mindedness. She said, "One thing that cheers me enormously is the barefaced confidence with which St. Peter says, "Lord, thou knowest that I love thee,' even though not many days later he denied him three times.

You'd think he might have curled up in a damp ball, moaning, 'Oh, I've really ruined everything this time…what will he think of me…it's all very well to say I'll never do it again, but why should he believe that…oh no, I'll never be able to look him in the eye again…"

But not St. Peter. With true apostolic verve, he bounces right back. Bold as brass he made his claim, counting not on his own proven weakness but on the character of his Lord, whom now, at last, he knew.

On those days when everything I touch turns to guilt and gloom and my heart lies limp as a fish within me, I think of St. Peter and mutter stubbornly, "Lord, thou knowest that I love thee."

"I'm not so sure, myself, but Lord, thou knowest."

The uncertainty of our actions is with us all especially in unexpected circumstances. But to continue through life with the notorious habit of talking and acting and reacting before thinking was, for me, inexcusable. Some attempt had to be made to change the course and some effort had to be made to reverse the doing and thinking syndrome—to thinking and then, reinforced by serious thought, doing.

To follow the leading of my own ideas—to practice being a thinker in order to become a thinker did not, at first, appeal to me. I didn't have proper credentials. It was unbecoming. Shades of conceit, I thought! No one seeks to become a thinker. One seeks to meditate, to evaluate, to analyze, to probe. Yet these remained merely by-products of thinking. I had to go for the big thing and I wanted to—I wanted to become a 'thinker.'

The first cold question hit me. Do I have the stuff of which a thinker is made?

Throughout our marriage my husband and I have taken many and various types of psychological tests. We have also given them and taught courses from them. I already had some information concerning my ability to think. One test was especially helpful for it revealed me to be a practical thinker more than a theoretical one; that is, I think more in pragmatic terms rather than abstract terms. From the content of a book I capture the story line but often lose the underlying message or meaning. In plays I enjoy the acting and casting, but miss the nuances and symbolism. In music, I hear the melody and the harmony but am often deft to the tone qualities finely demonstrated in individual instruments, plus the mood each measure exposes.

Jay Thomas, in his BiPolar Program, helps adults break the chain of non-awareness by emphasizing another attribute of one's character. His theory proposes that if a person is short on abstract thinking for instance, then that person could utilize a trait that is stronger in order to balance the less prominent or weaker trait. In my case my basic strength was independence. Independence denoted a natural recognition of self-confidence which meant, according to his theory; if I used this self-confidence appropriately it would beef up my weaker trait of theoretical thinking. My self-confidence then said, through my independent actions, I could become an abstract thinker. So jumping to an over-simplification of this program I, indeed, began to rely on my independence to become a better thinker.

Abbe Ernest Dimnet tells us that one of the characteristics of a thinker is his obvious vision. A thinker is a person who sees where others do not. Independently he finds this out as he refuses to accept the givens in situations and study. Who says I must accept the worn-out concept that the earth is flat, say Columbus? Let me go see for myself. Who says I must accept what others think of the musical Godspell? Let me go hear it for myself. Who says I must approve of the laws that are handed down by the Legislature? Are these men and women gods? Who says I have to accept the future as it comes to me? Why can't I make a difference?

Without further guidance I struck out to become an independent thinker—not necessarily a revolutionary thinker, but a thinker bearing the sole responsibility of my being and my doing. The lessons I was to learn astonished me and the keys I used to unlock the process in my mind could well be helpful to anyone whose mind is also restless for independent thinking.

I began to read differently. I began to study not only for the story line or for the point of the article, but I plunged into writing techniques, ideas that lay embedded in the text, hidden as they were, but placed there to push the point of the story further home. A world of knowledge is in the sub flow or underpinnings of each novel and many current writings. To be independent in my thinking meant I had to now search for the voice behind the voice of the writer myself and not allow some commentator or newspaper columnist or critic to speak and think for me. I had to begin by reading things I did not necessarily agree with on the surface.

On the plane coming from Florida one summer I found a Reader's Digest. It had been ages since I had read the Digest cover to cover. No doubt, lack of time as well as other interests robbed me of that pleasure; but this time, knowing I had two hours in captivity aboard the aircraft I set out. I read first all the articles that caught my fancy. These were fun. They read fast and were probably as quickly forgotten. Then I turned back and began reading the articles that didn't appeal to me, which I felt would be helpful. Rarely, I discovered did I read material that didn't have a natural appeal or emotional lure. This experience of reading what didn't catch my interest was an act of independence—not dependent on my feelings or emotions. Not only did I learn a great deal about subjects I didn't at first care about (the Digest has a marvelous faculty for addressing the current issues in concise cogency), but I had the thrill of broadening my base of knowledge and interest. New information was coming from directions from which I had previously closed my eyes and ears. Now with this act I made a scissor-step forward toward becoming a thinker.

Today, I can short circuit the process somewhat and proceed immediately to articles that hold secondary appeal. I find, at no surprise to anyone, a natural consequence of this experiment, my taste changing and my world enlarging.

Ernest Campbell once told me of a friend of his who took on a new subject each year. This year it's architecture, another year it was political science, another anthropology. This friend reads everything the libraries have on the subject and at the end of the year, he may not be an expert but he's knowledgeable enough to make valid contributions within the discipline. Many minds I respect and admire have this universal lure. Albert Outler, a man of world eminence in theology, is also an expert on loblolly pine trees. Can you imagine what my mind would be like if I filled my head with philosophy or etymology. Vast information may not be wisdom but knowledge fairly borne can do wonders to stretch one's ability to think and apply what we know, through discovery, to better our actions.

To read for content and ideas is far harder than I first imagined. I preferred to read from writers who could give me the dope in simple language and in digest form. My problem had been I didn't want to think. I much preferred being thought for, spoon fed, as it were, my knowledge predigested and made easy going down. Since this was so simple I often regarded what they said and wrote as gospel. I didn't take the time or expend the energy to do the thinking myself. This is mostly true with my experience with poetry writers. If I didn't understand their message on first reading, I'd turn the page. To tell the truth, I would still like to, but am learning and because I am on this kick of thinking independently, I am taking more time to ponder what has been written in what I call oblique language in order to curry out the meat that might be found there. Some recognize it instantly. I wanted to learn to do likewise.

The same is true of plays. Mingled in and out of the dialogue of plays is a story told by actors that conveys the message overtly and covertly by the author. If your experience is like mine,

I generally understand more about the play after the reviews come out than I do when I watch it. Someone else has gleaned an interpretation for me, the fine points and the telling theme that I often overlooked or I lacked the sensitivity to recognize it. I needed to shore up my senses if I was to be an independent thinker. To hear doesn't mean I've heard, to see doesn't mean I understand, to appreciate the enjoyment does not mean I have gained some revelation and internalized the message.

Not long ago I was pushed into a situation in which I had to attend a play that I didn't know was even playing. It was one of those topsy-turvy days when the day was planned one way and turned out another. At the time I had not begun to practice receptivity so I went to the play very unwillingly. The play was the classic Aria da Capa by Edna St. Vincent Millay and I can tell you since seeing it my life has never be the same.

As you may know the play is both a comedy and a tragedy. Two shepherds make up the bulk of the cast, and the story is told in mythical language, as the two herdsmen tend their flocks on the hillside. The two shepherds become bored with their jobs and decide to play a game. They draw an imaginary line across the field separating their property and their sheep. As the story develops the imaginary line becomes a wall and the tension of doubt, subterfuge and greed blind their judgments until the two friends become competitive, distrusting and selfish.

Soon the game they were playing to pass the time of day becomes the death knell for the two of them and they kill each other in their folly.

The obvious parts of the play came clear on the first viewing, but the play had undertones and overtones that preyed on my mind for days. In fact, I was so intrigued by it I used it as an example in a speech I gave a few weeks later on walls we build that are often invisible, yet set like a city fortress separating people and opportunity.

Before long I was at the library getting a copy of the play, and as I read it now with a purpose, many new ideas emerged— ones I had earlier missed in the dialogue, in the scene setting and in the underlying intent of the author. When I knew more about the play, I fell in love with it.

From that experience it came to me unless I am willing to make efforts toward becoming a thinker, I will miss, as I did on the first viewing of the Millay play, the truly great significant theme which was in this writer's mind.

The thought naturally followed, we are not put here to be sponges—to receive without response and live off the land wallowing in our pleasure. We are obligated, by our own gifts, to put back, to procreate in like fashion, consistent with our nature. To view any play, read any work of literature or study any work of art calls me to responsibility. I must receive that art with intelligence. I cannot do this without a mind free and independent, active and in the process of learning. I must compliment all artists and writers with a measure of appreciation that is not superficial, lazy or careless. To be knowledgeable demands appreciation in specifics. No longer should we tell a conductor his concert was entertaining. We must offer intelligent, concrete appraisal, "Especially beautiful was the Berlioz overture."

As I learned to be independent in my thinking, I was also aware I needed to think with purpose—to think with a reason. This whelped a whole new litter of ideas that surprised me, ones I had felt but had never formulated. Ideas beget ideas. If something is true, then logically something else must follow. Either inductive or deductive reasoning carries us through the full cycle of an idea, layering as it goes. The process of thinking then becomes its own art and is the stuff of which philosophers and theorists knead their daily bread.

I now asked myself what does the opposite point of view present? Or what makes one thing true and not the other? Philosophers have enjoyed this struggle and intellectual tug of war for centuries and I am just now learning that the thrill of becoming a thinker stresses the necessity of challenging each idea with another idea, testing it through the microscope of research and reason—from thesis to antithesis to synthesis.

This required a measure of concentration. Some people might call concentration the art of avoiding or the talent of being aloof—but whatever the term I have found the time to concentrate absolutely necessary. Some people go to extravagant extremes to learn to be quiet, and serene with their thoughts. Transcendental meditation, yogi, and many of the cults of reflection are appealing to some people because we are distracted and fragmented in the thinking process. I have found that to concentrate I must be interested in a given subject, but I also must have time, uninterrupted. If the interest is adequate and the time appropriate, the concentration process makes head way.

Not everything can hold our attention. I know this. Our judgment must come into play as to what deserves our attention. I am the first to confess certain subjects simply do not interest me. I have found, however, in time these might be the very subjects that I do have appeal. We learned earlier that time often changes taste. Therefore, I am more careful now than I used to be in regard to what is worthy or not worthy of my attention. I am beginning to believe, if not suspect, the more I become aware possibly everything is worthy, but just not yet timely or appropriate.

Thinking as a psychologist, one might dissect the mind into parts: here's the part that worries; here's the part that develops idea; here's the part that organizes behavior; here's the part that dictates motion; and here's the part that stimulates choice and will. All of them working simultaneously, and I find myself interested and disinterested at the same time. Since I am an inexperienced concentrator my interest span is understandably short, particularly if action is not immediate. My need to be up and at 'em often causes me to pass over or bypass the deeper significance of an idea or an event, much less the thought's nuances and dendrite extensions.

The power of concentration must come from within a person not from without. As I look around me this morning any number of things could keep me from concentrating—none of them would precipitate it—surely not the telephone, the books on my desk or the family passing by my door. But from within must come an interest, a love affair, even a slight one—like I am now having with that cricket over there by my door. Is it bad luck to kill a cricket? I am only nominally superstitious and lately we have been invaded with a new crop of crickets that hop their way into our house. Generally, my husband picks them up and flushes them down the commode. I am not that brave. I run for Raid. This little creature was raided to death. One spoof and he was gone, only as I noticed and watched... not immediately. I sat here at my desk and watched him. As the spray fell he did not move, obviously assessing his options. He knew he didn't feel normal. He tried to brush off the odd feeling with his front feet and tried to clear his eyes by rubbing them. His back feet became numb so he ventured a kick and a hop. He reared up on all fours and then twos, as if pleading like a praying mantis. I felt bad. Do I hurry and take him out of his misery or do I watch. I watch. A few seconds now of fitful flipping and flapping his wings and legs and the cricket is still. One last lunge turned him over, his legs cycling in the air, and then still again. I waited. This was it. He was dead.

Now thirty minutes later he is lying in repose on the carpet under the chair three feet from me. Had I not written of him, I surely would have forgotten him before noon. But this creature held my concentration for several minutes and now even longer as I write. The point is not to evaluate my moral attitude concerning death or my right or lack of right to kill him, but what was it that held my eyes and interest to him? I suggest my own inward struggle.

As I probed into my own learning process my being became clearer. You see, it helps to know what I am like in reflecting other things, other ideas and other people. What I was interested in learning and thinking about stemmed from my own innovations, creative aspirations and previous commitments to ideas. I had long since learned that I liked to read about things that agree with my prejudices. Yet, education must be to the whole person not something in the realm of the mind or a Teilhard De Chardin called the noosphere—that unexplained continuous layer of thought in motion around the earth. My learning and thinking came from within my own talents and reached the boundaries of my own imaginations—not some others imposed upon me. I found as I brought myself into focus with some small piece of the world, I was growing in my thinking. The encounter with the unthought of, the untried, the untested was an experience in itself, and brought further inspiration and motivation. As I thought, I did not grow up—I grew deeper.

From this came the marvelous discovery that thinking does not take place in a vacuum. It comes from an encounter! There must be a dialogue or a relationship with something else to effectively motivate proper thinking. Take my idea of becoming by being, for instance. For days I thought it was a good idea but I couldn't be sure until it encountered something, until I talked about it to someone or until it found a situation in which it could be used, exposed or developed. This happens in my reading of other people's ideas. A book is not merely a group of words stuck together on pages; it's an encounter. Anything that causes an encounter then is a source and opportunity for thinking and thus learning. Whatever the eye meets, a cloud, a worm, a speck of dust, this is an encounter and a provocation for thinking and deepening the learning process. Whatever the ear hears, a whistle, a sigh, a murmur, a gasp is an encounter and this prompts and promotes thinking and learning. My fear of becoming a thinker is to become one for my sake alone. A pitfall indeed. This is self-indulgence and a form of intellectual incest. To enjoy my own ideas is acceptable only as I fit them into the world of which I am a part. For my ideas like everyone else's must be tested by fire sparked from the critic's mind, and the results examined by research and reflection. I think ideas without communication are useless and senseless. They are sterile and worthless to me, as well as to the non-receptive world. One must move from an isolated position into a new and unexplored position that encompasses a larger field of creativity.

In Annie Dillard's delightful book written from Tinker Creek, she describes coming around a corner and suddenly encountering a bird falling to the ground. "The mockingbird took a single step into the air and dropped," she said. "His wings were still folded against his sides as though he was singing from a limb and not falling, accelerating thirty-two feet per second, through the air. Just a breath before he would have dashed to the ground, he unfurled his wings with exact deliberate care, revealing the board bars of white, spread his elegant, white-bank tail, and so floated onto the grass." The point she makes is that things like this are happening everywhere. "The fact of his free fall was like the old philosophical conundrum about the tree that falls in the forest. The answer must be, I think, that beauty and grace are performed whether or not we see or sense them. THE LEAST WE CAN DO IS TRY TO BE THERE!"

So I agree with Moustakes that any subject matter or environmental resource that extends knowledge and deepens appreciation and understanding is an appropriate source of enrichment and discovery. Each person is capable of wide ranges of experiences that serve to open and awaken him into new avenues of expression. What happened to me is what can also happen to you. As I purposed to become a learner as did Moustakes before me, new powers, new surges of feelings were created—imminently, immediately, intensely, vividly; and I as a person respond, talk back and engage in strange but unique dialogue as I reach out to touch life in new ways often for the first time. As I do, I see life in new colors—with the vast variation of composition; in sound—with its inexpressible vibrations and tones; in texture and touch in unknown regions; in ideas sailing freely in and out of my mind; in taste coming alive in awareness. As we participate in the thinking and learning process, we begin to reach out to meet other human beings with a clarity and fullness that creates a rhythm between the extremes of being and feeling.

Thinking does something to us. Heretofore I had the feeling that much of what was important depended on accomplishments and that my satisfactions were derived doing rather than on contemplation and being. I soon and happily learned what thinking for myself was doing to me. It was changing me. Not radically as fire changes matter to ashes, but over time more like the sunrise lifting imperceptibly into the morning.   I began to cherish those times when the natural thrust of my mind broke the traces of the givens and I could let it roam and romp free of the walls that used to scare me.   I fell in love with the meditative life, often sitting at my desk at 8 a.m. to ponder an idea, discovering ten minutes later it was noon. The thrill of working through an idea must be compared to the master bridge builder who places the final touch on his creation and opens the way for the world to pass over. To say it is fun may be trite, but the satisfaction and contentment defies all measure of pleasure.

So from these shaky first steps in my own history of becoming is found my study taking a new course. My future is still not fix. I am still working on it and having the time of my life. Who is to say what my tomorrow will bring? No one.

God and I have not decided yet.

THE STEP ABOVE

*O*ne of the grandest gifts a person can have is the sense of the exhilaration when the horizons of our lives expands and rises above the timber line of being. A new becomer's vision is restricted by doubts, lack of courage and hazy goals in the lower stages of his ascent, but these fall behind and dwindle as he climbs higher. At last, in the moment of becoming, the whole world is spread at his feet.

Encouraged and genuinely excited about becoming, though it may be in small accomplishments, my mind turns again to the fabulous freeways. I know some people think these long strips of asphalt are tree gobblers and landscape eye sores, but these modern wonders of transportation continue to serve illustratively in moments toward becoming. They lure us as a magnet and free our minds to literally zoom beyond the immediate and mundane.

Analogous to becoming are the engineering marvels these freeways are as they stretch forward and appear endless. Neither our sight nor imagination can see the roads' true courses, or their ultimate destinations. But we trust them. And staying with them we finally arrive at where we want to be.

The symbolism of the highway and its universality, as well as its transcendence, verges on the spiritual. A sermon given by Samuel Miller, a former dean of the Harvard Divinity School, reminds us that a man of faith is bound to be a man on his way, a visitor, the eternal "sojourner on earth" who has here below "no abiding city." He knows not; he believes. He has not; he hopes for. He sees not; he obeys. And his road is not defined like the unvarying orbit of a star...it is created under the feet of those who take it.

We make our own roads. And from the eidetic images that come to us on the highway we learn to appreciate the need and value of the feeder roads.

There is no more fitting description of launching into becoming than to understand the role of the feeder road. Each of us feed into the process what we want to become. I started with patience and I fed patience into the larger concourse of becoming. The momentum energized by the process took patience and moved it forward. We see the way now. The need to become connects with the feeder, the feeder to the mainstream and the mainstream to the total traffic toward wholeness.

Three of the feeder roads appropriate for the journey toward wholeness are self-discipline, selflessness and self-confidence.

Diligence takes self-discipline: the impetus to say 'no' when we would like to say 'yes' instead; the energy to stay seated when we are prone to jump up and catch the first car backing out of the driveway; the inclination to stick to the subject when our minds wander during desk chair ruminations. Diligence takes all the self-discipline we can muster. It checks our erratic desires and reins them into closely guarded routines. Left alone, we will waste time like a political filibuster, but by applying diligence, governed by self-discipline, we are kept steadily moving until at last we have crossed the finish line.

Selflessness points out the double aspects of becoming: believing and behaving. As much as we believe in the process, our behavior toward patience does not come unless it is chaperoned by a stricter motive. Patience demands selflessness. No way can we be selfish and wind up behaving patiently. The two simply do not operate in relationship.

By the same token self-confidence provides us with the stimulus and comfort to strive to become a better thinker. As we know, self-confidence is the inner assurance of worth and the appreciation of one's talents and abilities. It provides the courage to take our lights out from under the bushel, and place them in the center of our activities. Often, my self-confidence sulks too long in the backdrop of my being and must be brought to the forefront.

When it does, it merges with my desire to be a thinker and together the process allows the chance of my becoming one.

Before I leave my analogy of the road, I think it's an appropriate juncture to mention one more impulse that rumbles within the pit of our being that can be described only as 'motion.' Paul Tournier calls it a dominate factor and says that every one of us has a remarkable persistence which permeates our whole life from childhood onward and imparts unity to it. This motion, underscoring all that we think and do moves us outward into the ultimate beyond and connects us to the infinite potential waiting for us.

Motion, of course, is that silent movement within that has special relationship to change. It is the degree to which we acknowledge aliveness, to which we steep ourselves in the ongoing of the world and to which we link ourselves to the other active relationships. We are learning that all things are in motion and even the smallest forms operate in relationship. Edward Lindaman, a research scientist, in talking about wavicles, explains that relationship is true in the smallest element of matter. The wavicle is a combination of waves and particles that were discovered when splitting the atom; and they have identity only as they relate one to the other and are thus combined and appropriately called "wavicles."

We have tested and acknowledged the reality of our bodies, our emotions and our mental capacities, but there is still that prodding spiritual drive—that part of a person that is aware of an inner longing. Perhaps, it can best be described as the 'gift within,' that prevailing sensitivity of each of us to work to become our ultimate being...

> ...the motion of the hidden fire
>
> That trembles in the breast...
>
> John Montgomery

...that orders life to be lived from within...out!

It was this inner stirring that Magda Proskauer talked about when she began describing her own growth experience. She said, "My present approach to human growth is the outcome of early childhood experiences. When I was young, I loved to skate. Once the river in my home town was solidly frozen, I spent every free minute on the ice. As my body glided effortlessly it seemed I was carving handwriting on the mirrorlike surface. After I practiced ardently for hours, all restraint fell away, and a smooth shift of balance brought with it a sense of weightlessness. The joy of life that flowed through me in those days has never been forgotten. Thinking of it years later evoked the question: what is it that releases life?

"In those early experiences was a first realization of discipline leading to spontaneity, of effort leading to effortlessness. In those frosty hours, tireless concentration led to the kind of delicate balance that is a prerequisite for figure skating. Once the will power had been summoned to provide the skill, the same power could be shed; nature took over once more, so that genuine movement came through, bringing the sort of release I was looking for unconsciously. The spontaneous motion brought with it the 'e-motion of joy, of being fully alive.'"

Magda Proskauer has described 'faith in motion' or more precisely faith as motion. "Faith," said Bunyan, "cannot sit still; faith is forcible." To this, he adds, "faith is a principle of life by which a Christian lives, a principle of motion by which the soul walks forward toward heaven in the way of holiness."

Many years ago Walt Disney filmed a television special telling the story of the American eagle. Since too few people ever see eagles or witness their life or follow the habits of the huge American bird, it was fascinating to watch one soar through the heavens, even if it is on TV.

High on craggy cliffs, the large birds build their nest out of reach of any living creature and out of sight of the naked eye. As their young grow to the time of independence, it is thrilling to anticipate with the young eaglets the adventure that is soon to be theirs. They will leap from their nest and flap their wings. With one fell swoop they will learn to fly. No doubt, they question the wisdom of it all—can they do it? What would happen if they couldn't? Will their wings hold them and will their strength be sufficient? The moment, nevertheless, comes. The young eaglet is psyched for the occasion. The mother eagle prods…and he is off. Miracle of miracles, the young eagle dips into the wind, cutting the expanse with his wings, then pilots his body upward to the heavens. He is not disappointed in his wings or his strength. He discovers that the air itself supports him and buoys him upward, undergirding him and lifting him to the heights.

This is faith, the indescribable support, the unanticipated motion and strength, the surprising buoyancy that lifts us onward and upward to our own personal heights. The silent motion called faith pushes us out of our warm, secure, comfortable nests and forces us into a new adventure. It is exploring the newness of being in the realm of possibility.

As the faith of an eaglet is tested when he breaks from the nest, I find no richer definition of harmony than his launching. His wings catch the current and attest to the unity of all creation. What we are in search of, then, is a sequence of cause and effect so universal in its nature as to include harmoniously all possible variation of individual expression.

When the forces in our lives work together to produce harmony, the stage is set for flying—for our becoming free to be. When the individual is free to be himself, his acts are always consistent with his values and this is wholeness.

Many cultural conditions could well hamper or deny freedom, but we must not curb the personal freedom that is a divine right of all human beings. We may legally be controlled from driving a hundred miles an hour on the highways, but there is no legislation that can limit our personal freedom of becoming as we speed toward wholeness. Since it is real, it cannot be denied. Loren Eisley writes, "I have seen a tree root burst a rock face on a mountain or slowly wrench aside the gateway of a forgotten city…A kind of desperate will resides even in a root." So it is with us root becomers. There seems to be an inner drive, be it silent nudges, moving us constantly on course and directing us toward wholeness.

Yet the essence of wholeness must be considered today and not left for future happenstance.

Halford Luccock reminds us of a story written by Osbert Sitwell entitled, The Man Who Lost Himself. In it is a scene where the hero is trailing a person in Paris. He wanted to know if the man he was following was stopping at a certain hotel. He figured out that one way to do it without causing suspicion would be to ask the clerk of the hotel if he himself—giving his own name—was registered there. Then, when the clerk was looking at the register, he could glance down the page and see if the name of the other man was entered.

He carried out his plan and then got the shock of his life! The clerk looked up and said, "Yes, he has been waiting for you. He is in Room 40. When the man went into the room, there he found a man remarkably like himself—a little more gray, a little heavier, but undeniably himself. The person he met was himself as he would be at the age of forty, just twenty years ahead.

The story is fanciful or is it? Do we shudder when we think of ourselves in twenty or thirty years? Luccock points out, there is only one real way we can get a line on the kind of person we will be. We can do a lot of guessing or wishful thinking, but to be honest the only true line is by projecting, as in an architect's drawing, the lines on which we are now going. And he asked the next obvious question. Are our directions and habits worthy enough to continue for twenty years?

There is no royal road to discovering what we most want to become. Becoming is not a matter of when, it is lifetime intent that grows and magnifies in importance as time marches on. The intent of becoming is not static, like a process of growing up, it takes dips and dives; it is a process of testing and rejecting; of holding fast to that which is good and clinging to that which is even better. It is a process of curiosity and adventure, a seesaw process of high enthusiasm dropping at times to unexplainable disillusions. There are days when the going is great and becoming makes strikes of advancement, then there are other days, the down cycles I call them, when hopelessness scores and glories in it. On those days we must beware of false conclusions.

For instance, our youngest son mowed lawns for the summer to make money for next year's school activities. He soon was aware as he mowed, cleaned out the flower beds and trimmed the hedges, that within a week's time the weeds and crabgrass grew back and the yard looked as shabby as before. What he had just done had to be done again in a matter of days as surely as the sun peeked over the eastern horizon every summer morning.

This bit of hopelessness bear reflection. The process of cutting and grooming the lawn is not all that wasteful though it is definitely monotonous, for out of the ground comes nourishment. This is also true of becoming. Nothing is wasted. Out of the seeming nonsense, innocuous days, and repetitious experiences are formed our dispositions—the US that we call ourselves. And from natural nourishment comes periods of beauty and perfection.

Few ever desire to be a saint—much less call themselves working toward that end. Those who have obtained the honor never dreamed they would or should. Surely, they would be the first to veto the motion that their name be mentioned for elevation to such a high distinction. Sainthood is always a surprise.

It is awesome. Yet all are called to be saints, if we properly understand the word and meaning of sainthood as to be the best within us. No one can count themselves to have attained, but each is encouraged to seek excellence.

As we rise through our ventures in becoming, let us not miss this final crowning step. Let not false modesty cast a shadow of improper aspirations, but let us boldly tackle the art of saintliness as the height of all becoming. Certainly, true excellence is measured by a judgment far greater than our own. We can not canonize ourselves or present ourselves as saints. This would not only be unbecoming, it could cancel out the very qualities that make for sainthood in the first place. If we feel to become a saint is too erudite, maybe becoming a person of quality or becoming kind and generous might be a fair beginning. Which ever route appeals to us as an ultimate goal; no one achieves it as an illusion of the sweet by and by, but by working and living in the nasty and corrupt here and now.

There is a haunting story of a poor undernourished priest working in the slums of London. Someone asked him, "Why is it that you work down here among the filthy and deprived of the world." His answer, "I am here that the rumor of God may not be lost."

The becomer, who deliberately links his life to the suffering of the world, becomes in order to serve. No task is too mundane. To wash dishes, as did Brother Lawrence, or mow the grass or sweep out the jails or carry out bedpans is never too menial nor beneath the person who gives himself to humanity in the form of one-to-one relationship. To this becomer, a person is always a person of worth though the person may add up to be a community of people.

This gives us the idea that saints are made out of the stuff of which we are, those striving to be the best we can be—ordinary human beings living with ordinary human beings doing ordinary things. But they do it with love, absorbing the weaknesses and shortcomings of others unto themselves.

Therefore becoming by being is a spiritual quest rising out of a deep hunger and reaching out to all things in harmony and ultimate relationship. Listen to Pamela Frankau's statement: "There must come a time when...all your mirrors turn to windows." She then responds, "When we are young we are surrounded by mirrors, and wherever we turn we see ourselves. As we grow up the mirrors dissolve, and the windows that replace them set our horizons free. We learn to see people as they see themselves, to understand the complexity, the shifting, the light and shadows of other people's lives and emotions and through understanding them understand, in some measure, ourselves. We realize that nothing is as simple as it looks in the mirrors, but that everything is far more wonderful. And finally, we learn the most marvelous truth of all: that, in the last analysis, we can never know the whole truth about anyone or anything, but that we are, like Tennyson's Ulysses, a part of all that we have met."

It is said of Eisenhower that when he was called in to organize the Allied forces for the invasion of Germany he went before the selected staff. They were gathered around a very big table loaded down with stacks of papers. The task looked hopeless. Eisenhower looked at the staff a few moments and then to the table and said. "Well, let's begin here."

If today we are kind, our tomorrow will be different for us. If today we are fair, our tomorrows will be harmonious. If today we are generous, gratitude will catch the wind and the whole world will ultimately sing.

BIBLIOGRAPHY

Assagioli, R. The Act of Will, New York: The Viking Press. 1973.

Barclay, W. Daily Celebration. Waco: Word Books. 1971.

Barnes, K. The Creative Imagination. London: George Allen and Unwin LTD. 1960.

Boom, C. The Hiding Place, Washington Depot, Conn., Chosen Books.1971.

Bruner, J. On Knowing, Cambridge: Harvard University Press. 1963.

_____ A Study of Thinking, New York: Science Editions, 1967.

Clinebell, H. Jr. The People Dynamic, New York: Harper and Row.1972

Chute, B. When the Writer Comes of Age. Writer, November.1966.

De Chardin, P.T. The Appearance of Man, New York: Harper and Row. 1956.

Dillard, A. Pilgrim at Tinker Creek, New York, Harper's Magazine Press. 1974.

Dimnet, A. The Art of Thinking. New York: Simon and Schuster. 1936.

Dubos, R. A God Within. New York: Charles Scribner's Sons.1972.

Drury, M. The Inward Sea. New York: Doubleday.1972.

Ensley, F.G. Persons Can Change, Nashville, Tenn: The Graded Press, 1963.

Erickson, E H. Identity, Youth and Crisis, New York: W. W. Norton, 1968.

Fromm, E. The Art of Loving, New York: Harper and Row, 1956.

_____, Man from Himself, New York: Rinehart, 1947.

Hamilton, J. W. What About Tomorrow, Old Tappan, New Jersey: Fleming H. Revell, 1972.

Hawthorne, N. The Great Stone Face, New York: Houghton Miffin, 1882.

Jordan, C. The Day I Decided to Do It Myself, Guidepost: September, 1973.

Keen, S. Golden Mean of Roberto Assagioli, Psychology Today: December, 1974.

LeShan, L. How to Meditate, New York: Bantam Books,

1974.

Lewis, C. S. Mere Christianity, New York: Macmillan, 1943.

Luccock, H. Unfinished Business. New York: Harper and Row, 1956.

Marney, C. Priest to Each Other, Valley Forge: Judson Press, 1974.

Malania, F. The Quality of a Hazelnut, New York: Alfred A. Knopf, 1968.

May,R. Love and Will, New York:W. W. Norton, 1969.

Michener, J., The Quality of Life, New York: W/W.Twentyfirst Corporation, 1970.

Millay, E. Aria de Capa.

Moreno, J.L. Who Shall Survive. New York: Beacon Press, 1953.

Moustakes, C. The Self, Explorations in Personal Growth. New York: Harper and Row, 1956.

Nidetch, J. Weight Watchers, New York: W/W Twentyfirst Corporation, 1970.

Otto, H., Guide to Developing Your Potential. New York: Charles Scribner's Sons, 1967.

Parker, W. P. Prayer Can Change Your Life, Englewood Cliffs, N.J: Prentice-Hall, Inc. 1957.

Potthoff, H., A Whole Person in a Whole World, Nashville: Tidings, 1972.

Powell, J., A Reason to Live! A Reason to Die! Niles, Illinois: Argus Communications, 1972.

_____ Why Am I Afraid to Love? Chicago, Illinois: Argus Communications, 1976.

Rutledge, H. In the Presence of Mine Enemies, Old Tappan, New Jersey: Fleming H. Revell, 1973.

Seabury, D. The Art of Selfishness, New York: Julian Messner, 1964.

Shaw, G. B. Saint Joan. New York: Modern Library.

Sparks, R. Today, Millere Music Co.

Williams, Margery, The Velveteen Rabbit. New York: Doubleday, 1958.

Thomas. J. W. Your Personal Growth, New York: Frederick Fell, Inc. 1971.

Thoreau, H.D. Walden, Cambridge: The Riverside Press, 1957.

Tournier, P. The Person Reborn, New York: Harper and Row. 1966.

BECOMING BY BEING

www.ingramcontent.com/pod-product-compliance
Lightning Source LLC
Chambersburg PA
CBHW031339040426
42443CB00006B/390